The whole package woman

by

Rebeca Petran

Table of content

Introduction
Mindset
Spirituality
Health
Relationships
Wealth

Bonus Chapter

Chapter I

Introduction

As I look at this blank page, I cannot help but wonder how to start writing this book? What is the best method of opening to a non-fiction book where the intention is to inspire others to be better? Statistics and research might be the answer, but I chose to do it differently.

First of all, I want to say thank you for picking this book up and I am sure you will get exactly what you need out of it!

I, also feel like I want to introduce myself and shake a hand, but I guess it's not the case.
As you assume, I am known for my jokes

I believe life is meant to be fun and joyful, so you will find my funny escapades throughout the book.

You might be a friend that decided to read this book because of my persuasion or you might be a family member that wants to support me and my dreams or you could be the person that received the book as a recommendation, I want to thank you all!

Each one of you that picked this book up and read it, I am really grateful for spending your priceless time on reading my work. I aim to get you inspired, influenced and motivated in any way possible- that is the reason why I decided to write a book on how to become a better person.

Thank you and enjoy it!

Having said that, now, I am going to make a short introduction and tell you exactly what you will discover throughout the book.

For me to present the whole book, the content and how will it benefit you from reading it, I want to say thank you to the person that inspired me the most in my life. My mother. She is the ultimate whole package woman and I haven't met anyone like her. She overcame terrible situations, diseases, carried 2 children, has been a single mom, studied, bought property on her own, joggled 2 jobs at the time, started and managed businesses; all this, whilst raising her kids, taking care of herself and always looking impeccable, helping members of family and making time for leisure. As much as this seems to be successful and it is, she had to sacrifice plenty to be able to offer her kids something better than she had.

Mum, I love you and thank you! You have been a real inspiration.

So, the whole package woman- this book it's created to learn more about yourself, to get that positive vibration, to create a life vision according to you, to successfully follow through with a plan and to have a winning mindset no matter the circumstances.

The changes within yourself will happen so smoothly that you won't even realize how your whole perspective in life has changed and your chances of getting where you want to get have drastically improved.

I have got for you a combination of the best and most influential parts of all the training and coaching I have done.

So, what's in the book?

You will find a 5 step system that I have created and teach you how to use it to create a better life for yourself. The system we have now, it's the one that got us where we are; now we require a new software to update and upgrade. You will get transformed just by reading chapter by chapter. You will find yourself having more confidence, being clearer on what you desire, challenge yourself, take action towards your dreams and stick to your plans.

Now, I will let you think if it's worth reading further.

Let me give a little bit more inside on who I am.

I am a woman, a whole package woman, just like you. I am a foreigner, I live in the UK and I love sunny weather. I have had a bumpy ride until the last few years and I am really grateful for all those years of uncertainty and disappointments as I can stand in front of people now, knowing I overcame struggles and show others how to do it as well.

Moving on, no matter the outside opinion, nor circumstances, I never gave up on my dreams and I always looked ahead at what's possible; that is what got me to this exact point in life-to write a self-empowering book and to actually let people read it (believe me, that is the hardest part).

This book is not to preach you on how to live your life, nor to put myself on a pedestal; this is knowledge and experience I accumulated about the subject in matter. I have been deeply passionate about everything concerning mindset, overcoming issues, being better, creating a better life, etc. I am constantly looking for a new course, a new book and new people to listen to, so I can learn more about how to be and have better of everything.

I am grateful for how my life turned out to be and I cannot wait to see what's ahead.

Things haven't been always like this, as you can assume. I won't bore you with childhood details, but that particular time of my life shaped me, my personality and my beliefs.-many of which I had to consciously work on the subconscious in order to change.

I have been through physical violence, verbal abuse from my step dad's side and I have nearly lost my mum a couple of times because of his addiction and violent nature.

I have raised myself and my younger brother for a few years in high school, whilst taking care of a household and struggling with an eating disorder and extremely low self-esteem.

In a nutshell, all these events were 'supposed' to set me on a 'not so successful' path and they all influenced my attitude and character later on in life.

As much as I considered myself a victim back in the day, that changed in a moment. Maybe, you heard it before, but the idea of change happening in a moment, it's extremely real and I experienced it on myself. You can read as many books and go to as many seminars as you want to, but change happens within yourself in a second, and not through thinking about it. I switched my mindset in a moment, 6 years ago; after spending 2 days indoors, crying and pitying myself, I had a moment when I just felt like 'enough is enough'; I had enough of crying and punishing myself because of other people's issues.

I wish I could tell you I saw I bright light and I had an intense emotional moment, but I didn't; the only thing I felt was excitement, that kind of feeling where you feel indestructible.

After that day, nothing has ever been the same. I looked for therapists, I started reading books, I started buying courses and took a decision of changing my life.

Now, I am more than happy to say that all my relationships with my family are great and me and my stepdad can sit down, enjoy a coffee and have a normal conversation. I have been doing courses and coaching to learn how to help others, I started a property business, I wrote this book and the most important thing: I got over trauma, I build my confidence up, I have learned what self-love is, I forgave people who wronged me and my loved ones and I realized how meaningless life is without dreams and a clear purpose.

As you will see later on, this book has nothing to do with my life story explained above; this book is technical and step by step organized in order to achieve the 'whole package' rank.

The book was an idea I had about the areas of life and how we can work around them, so we don't neglect any and manage them to achieve a high level of success.

Over one year ago I was working with 2 relationship coaches and a life coach after a breakup I was just going through. I decided to do that because I knew I wanted someone to get me faster on track and with as little as possible damage to everything I have been working for until then. It was a 3-year relationship, so 3 people should've been enough (joke)

Said and done, they were great, a couple of months later I was following exactly what they advised me to, without any of their input.

That's when I found the glitch in the system.

Maybe you have heard of this before- your life being broken down in 3 areas: health, wealth, relationships. Really?

That's when I realized: It's not just that! at all.

I was there, having worked with relationship coaches and life coaches to get over a 3-year relationship, when all my friends would just eat ice cream, rant to everyone and watch sad movies, for months after that. I was there, taking action towards my dreams, planning next moves and following advice from the experts because I understood the importance of doing things for yourself and not giving up on what you desire.

It hit me; life is not just about those 3 areas! Life is more and I knew it! My reaction, my perception, and my actions were completely different than anyone else's. If my mindset wouldn't have been in the right place, I wasn't going to look for ways on how to ease that transition.

So, the main thing in absolutely everything in life is mindset.

A growth mindset is something that is created through beliefs, habits and actions. But, no other plan will work without being a spiritual person; I am not talking about going to church, praying, etc -not that is anything bad with that; I am talking about that inner connection to your true self and that centered, peaceful feeling, that some get while being present in a church, meditation, praying, reiki and so on.

So, my 5 step system is :

Mindset

Spirituality

Health

Relationships

Wealth

Now you understand the titling of the book: Mindset to Wealth; it is taking you through all these steps one by one.

This is how the whole package forms and you will see how it goes more in-depth through each chapter and you will learn from each statement and each exercise.

It is easy to read and understand, but the real changes will only happen when you actively take action towards the things you desire.

Believe in yourself, believe in your dreams, believe in your power and don't give up. Be an example for your kids and everyone else around you. Make others look at you and admire your determination and kindness, inspire people to live their best life under their terms; don't dwell on the past and constantly strive to be better and achieve those dreams that sometimes you don't even dare to share with the ones close to you.

Life is too short to wait for opportunities, for people making decisions for you, for standing in your bench waiting for others to see your hard work and skills. Everything is up to you and everything starts with you. The moment you get yourself 'together', become emotionally fit and start taking action towards your dream life, nothing will ever be the same; you will see the true power you hold and ultimately feel what fulfillment really is.

This book is the result of a lot of personal work, self-development, coaching, books, courses and many more. I have been working on myself intensely in the last few years and I have learned greatly. It was about time to give back and help others do the same.

I have been consciously changing myself, working on emotional issues, learning about myself and ultimately creating the person I want to be.

It's a never-ending process and I couldn't see life worth living without the chances and opportunities of being and doing better for me and everyone else. I am aware that we can not be perfect, but this is what makes me strive for better. We have been told that perfection cannot be reached and that cancer cannot be cured and there are still people looking for treatments and finding remedies for it. I am associating being your ideal you, the perfect self with an "incurable" disease. If people are not giving up by the fact that cancer can't be cured, why should we stop on making ourselves better, finding new solutions and new ideas to become the person we know we can be. We can be the best at what we decide to do; that's how we have champions, role models, medal winners and award achievers.

You will find yourself challenged a lot throughout this book, as there will be statements, interpreted quotes and questions, all specially designed to make you think and find your true answers.

Stop for a second and think why did you pick up this book. What was your expectation? To confirm the fact that you're a whole package woman? To learn something new on how to become one? To share some ideas with others? Or were you expecting some cheesy story?

Whatever your answer is, I am extremely grateful for you choosing to read my book and I am a hundred percent sure you will learn new things, challenge some fixed mindsets and start seeing your life with a defined purpose.

What is the whole package woman?

The whole package woman is whatever the heck she wants to be

That is the truth! That is the mindset! The whole package woman is absolutely anything that she desires to be because she wants to.

Who is a whole package woman?

Everyone is a whole package woman!

So now you're thinking 'why am I reading this then?' Well, because you are a whole package woman, but you don't know it yet.

What is a whole package woman? It is a combination of qualities, a series of contradictory features, a mix of traits that put together the wonder woman.

From being kind to sociable, from being sporty to glamorous, from active to chill and Netflix, from being independent to vulnerable, from silly to witty and everything else in between. The whole package woman consists of many physical, emotional and intellectual traits that complete and oppose each other.

The whole package woman can do and be whatever she wants to and is going for everything she wants in her life. She is not afraid of challenges, she is ready to take action, she follows her dreams, she lives her life according to her needs, she loves people and people love her, she apologizes when she should and she doesn't let herself brought down by others.

The whole package woman speaks her mind in a kindly manner, works smart and not hard, knows who she is and what she wants and she brings value to others by living her best life.

The whole package woman is a combination of strength and humility, independence and vulnerability, career-oriented but marriage material, fun and carrying, determined and kind, has a social life and loves time on her own.

That's definitely not the short and simple definition you were expecting.

When you have a look at the women you are inspired by, the role models in your life, the women you are following and that you would like to be like, I can guarantee one thing: all of them have more than one good trait. Maybe it's a movie star, a celebrity, an entrepreneur or someone from your own family. The woman you admire has maybe beauty, a great career, a beautiful family and all in between; because the amazing woman you would like to be like, has it all. When you really look into this, you discover that you have been looking up to people in your life that have more than one good trait; a person that has opposite characteristics because that is what we interpret as having it all. Just have a look at the cinema stars, the female characters that are being idolized: Lara Croft, Cleopatra, Wonder Woman, Katniss (the hunger games), Princess Leia, etc. All these females are being portrayed as an ideal woman. Understand why is that; when you look a little bit deeper and from a psychological point of view, you see that they portray an image of a beautiful, smart, courageous, generous, kind, strong, loving woman. The thing is that we let this decide that only those "unreal" characters can be that whole of a woman. We let others do the thinking for us and in that way we limit ourselves by believing that we can either have one or the other. It's BS. Anyone can be that!

You can have the amazing body, the business that you want, the family and the children you are dreaming of, without any compromise, just by having a clear vision of yourself.

Be the woman that can do anything, that is positive, smart, that respects herself and others, knows what she wants and has a can-do attitude.

All of the qualities mentioned above are mindset based because that's where it all starts and please see the fact that I mentioned qualities because all of them are.

You don't need to feel weak because you need someone else's help to do something, or needy because you can let a man take care of you; you can be and do all, with the right attitude; and be sure you will attract the right people around you after you find, create and model yourself.

Be a woman that has high goals and ambitions but receive help along the way, be independent and have a great career but let the right man serve you breakfast in bed.

Further along, starting now, you will see some clear statements and a detailed explanation after each one. It is structured in such a way so that these affirmations have an impact when first read and make sense when you go into more detail.

Chapter II

Mindset

Mindset

So what does mindset mean to you?

Mindset explained is very simple, mindset is a way of thinking. It is all about believing in something or not.

Just like this book: if you believe you will benefit from it and learn something, you will; if you have a fixed mindset and believe there is nothing else you can improve in your life, you won't even bother reading further.

Mindset is just the way you think, the way you look at life. "is just" makes it seem so insignificant; that is exactly what is not. Mindset is everything! It controls you, it determines your success or lack of it, it releases or holds your potential, it guides you through life.

"Whether you think you can or can't, either way, you're right! H. Ford

The simplest way to understand what mindset is.

Your thoughts, your thinking process, the way you talk to yourself, the subject that are preoccupying you; these are the things you need to pay attention to.

In your mind is where all of the creation is happening, that is the first step, so be careful what you spend your time thinking about. You can not picture getting the promotion and at the same time think about that envious colleague of yours having a breakdown over it; please have a pure heart and a clear mind.

You can not desire kids and having a happy family and at the same time judge other moms based on how they decide to raise their little ones. These are contradictory thoughts.

Envision and create the life you desire but stay away from negative feelings, emotions.

The way your mind works comes from your own experience to certain events in your life and the way you perceived your bringing up.

What makes us all different is the fact that we were raised in different cultures with other people's mentality and even if we would have similar childhoods, we would have different, personal, internal experiences; even if we were raised by the same people, we would become completely different personas because of the way our mind reacts to different scenarios.

There is no good or bad when it comes to the way your mind works, but you need to learn how to "control" it; and the only things you can be in control of are your focus, your reactions and the way you feel.

How many times did you find yourself saying you don't care about something but next minute getting anxious or stressed over it? How many nights did you waste going through a situation over and over again? How many times did you say something you didn't mean to someone you cared for? How many books did you start without finishing any? How many projects did you start just to give up when facing the first challenge?

I am here to tell you that you can change that.

The past is not a reflection of the future

As much as this speaks for itself, we still don't believe it on a subconscious level.

What happened in the past puts its fingerprint on us and it's driving us in future endeavors. We had negative and positive experiences and we created out of them, some beliefs that still operate today. It's like getting many layers of clothing.

One experience turns into a belief that would equal a T-shirt; another experience turns into another belief that becomes a top; something else happens to us which is a cardigan and so on;

To put it into a more realistic example: let's say you had a kid bully you when you were little-that experience created a belief. Someone may have categorized you in school 'not being good at sports' and that created for you another belief. The challenge is to start seeing these events and beliefs as something we wear daily unless you already identified and changed them. We all had life experiences until now that shaped us. The main thing to understand is that some of our beliefs are stopping us and some are driving us.

The real issue when it comes to that is the fact that most of our beliefs are negative. We do create loads of positive beliefs, but not as many as negative. So, picture yourself with 10 layers of clothing, 10 different beliefs about money, relationships, sexuality, spirituality, etc., and see how you go into the next job, next relationship, business and so on. The most important thing is that we have the power and the tools to change that and start living life as a blessing. I will show you how in another book, as there is a lot to cover on this subject.

To go back to our statement, it is important to understand how much we are influenced and guided by negative experiences. We need to realize how each particular event was an isolated one and stop giving it the power to drive us in our future adventures.

To identify those beliefs look at the ones I am mentioning below;

"life is hard", "Losing weight is difficult", "marriage is hard work", "all men are cheaters", "doing business with family is wrong", "people take advantage of you", "you need to work hard for money", etc.

We do create these beliefs out of the most ordinary examples and situations; it can go as deep as certain looking people start having a label in your head, or certain jobs to make you feel a certain way because you have a belief about that, and everything goes in a circle that won't stop until you put an end to it.

What happened is not what will happen. We logically may get it, but our subconscious mind will still operate from that belief until we take charge of it. The way to override the subconscious is by repetition and habituation. Pretty clear, start verbalizing the statement and create habits that are opposite to what you have been doing until now.

Good is a trap!

Who wants good in their life? Don't you want amazingly great in your life?

Stay away from that disease because it will trap you into a meaningless unfulfilled life! You can have a good life or you can have a great life. The choice is yours. You know how you would like your life to look like, but the more you choose normality, the less meaningful satisfaction will bring into your life.

Having a good job, a good house, good relationships, good pay-check says that you are just a 'good' type of person. It doesn't point out your uniqueness, doesn't release any bit of your potential, doesn't encourage any progress or growth. Do you want to be just good? Is that your definition?

Anyone can achieve a good state, a good marriage, a good job, ok health; are you that basic?

Don't fall for the 'good' type of things as they are a lie. As a first exercise just look at this scenario. Someone you know messages you and asks you how was your day. You immediately answer "it was good", "it was ok". I spoke to several people about this and they all confirmed this: you say it's 'good' or 'ok' when nothing happened, it was boring or actually, some things went in a different way than expected.

Based on this, we already define 'good' by not having excitement, happiness, fulfillment, drive and so many other positive feelings. If things would go exactly as expected in the day we received the message, if we have done something we are passionate about, if we have been working towards our dreams and goals, if we see ourselves closer to achieving certain things, your answer would definitely not be 'good'. And I will let you decide from now on, how are you going to answer that particular question and I hope it won't be 'good', as that will mean you are taking control of your life.

Start selecting the things that are good and great in your life and make a decision which way is your life going.

Average doesn't exist!

This goes hand in hand with the statement above.

If you take away something from this, take away that, make it the main statement in your head. We are so fricking amazing, each one of us and we don't even know it; what other reason would be for us to not live a fully fulfilled life than not knowing the amazing things we can achieve. Physically we have many resemblances to one another, but our minds, talents, skills are uniquely designed around our persona and that is our magic.

No one defined our potential, it is us taking those decisions through which we decide we cannot do or be certain things. Our potential is limitless, but we wouldn't know that unless we challenge ourselves.

There must've been times in your life when you have done something you didn't believe you could and were absolutely amazed by it, felt empowered, indestructible and like you can do anything else afterward.

Well, if you are here reading this you most probably overcame whatever you thought in the past it was unfixable. Whenever you get over something, fix a situation, do something you are scared of, you come out more confident, empowered, believing in yourself more and that is the state we want to be in at all times.

The way we work is like that; if you sit on the sofa and watch TV every day, don't expect to feel empowered or confident or to have a greater life; nothing will change from a state of comfort or acceptance of the current situation. Things change for you and your life when you challenge yourself; your current situation is the result of what have you been thinking and doing so far; your life ahead is not conditioned by your current reality; you can start from this moment to see that and start challenge this concept of 'average'.

Life is not a journey from when you're born to the moment you leave this earth. Your life has a meaning and you need to start looking for your purpose because there is nothing average about you or anyone else around you. Look at the ways you stop yourself from thinking big, chasing dreams, feeling like you are not good enough to get something in life and how ultimately, live a life of unfulfillment. No one is average, we just don't know what we can do and where we can get. As soon as you start realizing that, no mountain is too high to climb. It is one of the most important things, to understand that you are special in different ways and extraordinary is your fabric.

When you live your life without anything to look up to, feeling like you need to have special powers to achieve success in any area, that's when you start failing on yourself and others. The issue is not that you only stay where you are, dying, because you have no progress in your life, the problem is that you will influence others on doing the same.

You put negative ideas into the minds of the ones close to you, you start conditioning them to stick to their normality and don't strive for more in life.

Start seeing life as a domino effect. Each and one of us has the power to influence others, but when that happens with something negative, that doesn't bring value to other people is when you truly failed and your life hasn't been well lived.

Just think about that for a second.

Do you want the ones you love to have an amazing life, live happily and achieve their dreams? If you do, and you do, start being an example by living your best life, by chasing your dreams, by not putting limitations on your potential and continue moving and striving for something great.

Release your potential bit by bit and constantly ask yourself what else can you do. This is the way you will live an amazing life, will feel above average and influence the ones around you to do the same.

Everything starts with one idea; one belief. That is The Possibility!

This is the foundation of everything you desire; If you see the possibility of achieving those dreams or not. If you can desire one thing (or more) and believe that you can get it, you will find all the tools to get there and obstacles will be just a speed bump in the road that you pass over. If you think that certain things cannot be fructified, they will for sure not be obtainable for you; mainly because subconsciously you decided of un-achieving that particular dream, so you won't even look for the resources you might need.

When it comes to creating yourself, and this is what we are talking about in this book, possibility acts as the base; you have to see within yourself that you are capable of great achievements.

Is it possible to have that job that you want? Is it possible to reach that money figure? Is it possible to learn that skill you need? Is it possible to have that body? Is it possible to have that great relationship? Is it possible to become famous? Is it possible? The best question to ask yourself whatever it is you are thinking about. Is it really possible for you?

As a tip for anything you might be thinking about: if someone else has done it or has something that you want, you can be, do or have as well!

There is nothing new about this; I am just saying it in simpler words that I hope it will influence the way you look at your life.

Nothing will stand in the way of a person that believes it's an achiever!

Nothing will stand in the way of a person that believes in possibility!

You are your grand design!

The best way to start creating yourself is by imagining, picturing how you would be at your best.

Sounds simple, right? Well, it is, but not too many people are living up to their potential and they get lost along the way in activities, jobs, relationships and lifestyles that are not their idea or preference.

The starting point is who do you want to be? How would you like to look like? Who would you like to date? What job would you love doing? Where would you like to go on holiday? Would you like to have children or not?

The idea with the questions above is to make you start thinking about your perfect self, living your perfect life.

Perfect it really is a big word, because nothing is perfect, but the image you create for yourself and the vision you see for your life is perfect for you.

You need to create such a clear picture of what you want that no matter what happens in any area of your life, that picture will still be your focus. What I mean exactly is that your ideal self won't have time to wonder what other people think, you won't care about what others are doing because you will be so focused living the life you are creating.

When you start picturing your best self the emotions are the first part.

How would you feel?

The daily state you will be in. Take a second to think about that. You achieved those dreams, you are at the destination. How do you feel? You have to get into that state.

How would you be on a daily basis? The answer is pretty simple and hopefully, everyone thinks about being happy, fulfilled, joyful, grateful.

The challenge I am going to make you undertake is the one where you see that no dream is worth achieving if you go through life being negative and experiencing a low state of mind.

There is nothing more disappointing to me than to see people desiring certain things and instead of enjoying the process of getting there, they are miserable and stressed out; they are falling into that trap of self-pity and victimization. What is it so bad about their goals that makes them unhappy to take action and follow through? Your goals should empower you and make you a better person while you pursue them, not transform you into a miserable person that just does things for the sake of doing.

The feelings you have about the things you desire are the first factor in identifying what makes your heart smile and what doesn't. Start by doing that: identify what feels light and what feels hard and heavy; start making your own choices on what you desire out of life and who do you want to be. You will notice that the moment you will choose something that you want and that something feels like a job or you believe it's a 'rational' want, it's not really your passion and you will have trouble following through. You will have to choose the things that automatically put a smile on your face and you can't wait to wake up tomorrow morning to start working to get them.

Live life on a daily basis with the feeling that you already achieved everything you desire.

Dream big or don't dream at all.

Reassess your daily attitude on following your dreams; your state of mind should be positive and confident unless it's not your path that you are moving towards to. That should be your main clue on understanding that your dreams are yours to start with and that you are doing what your inner being is craving for. Dreams cannot be classified in any way, except at the beginning of the process as you will most probably see some of them being "too big". As soon as you start following one of them and see how much is worth it and that it might be even easy, they become "small" and another "big" goal it is set to be achieved. As it is always best to ask yourself "what else can I do?"

The power in that question is inexplicable as it sets your mindset on possibility and on the path of personal, achievable success.

The problem with setting 'achievable' goals is that there is no motivation for you to go after them; if you think that you want some extra money per month, or you just want that holiday this year, or anything else that you would classify as basic, realistic, is that you will not feel any excitement and willingness to pursue them. Who wants just that? Why limit yourself from the beginning of the process? You don't even know what you are capable of, yet you set a low target just to feel comfortable that you can achieve it. Well, guess what, you can achieve that theoretically small goal and you will understand that you could've set a higher one and achieve it in the exact same way; it's just that you didn't see the chances of getting there. Or there are the others that set basic targets just because they are afraid they will fail and be humiliated or judged.

Let go of that! People will judge you anyway, no matter what kind of things you set yourself to do! But the secret is: they don't matter.

Don't restrict yourself on the norms the others set for themselves; you, now, know better than that.

A big or a small goal, it's just our own interpretation that defines that. I find it that for myself the goals that make me jump out of bed and work for them, are just the ones that seem to be impossible to achieve. The more people around me say things like 'it's hard', 'it takes a long time', 'it's impossible', 'it won't happen for you', 'you can't have that', the more drive rises inside me. My inner voice even says "try me, beach". It doesn't mean people don't want me, you or anyone else achieve a considerable high level of success; they are just looking out for us not to get disappointed. And here is us coming in and saying "no one will be disappointed". Because we know we won't be dissatisfied by following our true nature and desires.

As soon as a goal is near to be fulfilled, a new one has to be set. The power and the energy of being nearly there is so fresh and pure that you don't want to waste it; the mind will only see the ways to get to your dreams and will find innovative ideas that you consciously cannot see. The reason we should set new goals as soon as we almost achieved one is because we are creatures that live by progress in life. Progress means being alive. Did you hear before the concept of what doesn't grow, dies? Well, the things that don't grow are the things that stay where they are, the things that haven't suffered any change, the things that have deep roots in any comfortable situation. By things, I mean people and the whole idea is to understand that even if you don't consider yourself regressing, that fact that you are staying in a situation without progress, makes you slowly degrade from many points of view.

Also, we have no idea of our own potential and the things we are capable of. Why not find that out?

Let's look at a gym exercise like running; if you are like me, you most probably don't really like running on the treadmill or anywhere else in fact, but the challenge to see how much I can do today and how much I can improve that time by in tomorrow's session is priceless. It's teaching you that you haven't been born to accept things as they are, is teaching your brain that you are in control of your actions and makes you unleash another bit of your potential. Don't quit setting new things up to achieve for yourself and don't stop dreaming, as you will slowly die.

We can see every day how famous people that we admire are coming from humble beginnings and do such amazing things now. What's stopping you? What is it that you have less than anyone else? What is it that you are missing that stops you from going after what you want in life?

I will answer that for you: you don't have the dream and the possibility mindset.

I once heard this quote "have a goal so high that is worth failing for" and it made me think about the meaning of it. At first, I was caught up in the failing phase, as to why should you have a goal that you are expecting to fail? But it means something different for me, it enforces my personal belief that goals and dreams should be really high, otherwise why would you even put energy or thinking about something basic? If it is to set a goal, a target, make it big, make it exciting, get thrills and chills when you think about it. That is exactly what is going to make you get out of bed, say no to meaningless nights out, turn off the TV and other time-wasting activities.

Choose your dreams carefully and make sure you put your energy into something big, that it is worth it, that is life-changing and adds value not just to you, but to everyone else around you.

Don't let your current situation determine your goal-setting process, as you will get limited. The reality you are experiencing now shouldn't limit the one you are stepping into. Make it big and make it your life purpose to achieve the things you are dreaming of. Like the commercial says "you're worth it".

What is it in your life right now it won't be there forever, even if it's great, even it's not like you are picturing it. If it is great, you will still have to put some effort into maintaining it that way, either is a business, a relationship or health. If your life it's not matching your desires, then you still have to actively work for what you want. You have no excuse. Just get it done!

So going back to that quote, the failure expression can be interpreted in many ways; if I wrote this book and it will be considered a failure by the majority out there, I am ok with it, because for me, if I managed to change someone's point of view on any subject presented onwards, I didn't fail. But if it will be seen as a 'failure' at least I failed at selling a book I wrote from scratch and it was worth it.

By my own life example, I hope the idea of having a goal worth failing for, it makes sense and it will also make you set goals worth failing for.

"A man's worth is no greater than his ambitions." M. Aurelius

Failure only happens when you give up!

After you set your high goals another thing to remember is that continuous action is required to get to the destination you set for yourself. If your dreams are worth your time and energy, failure will never occur. Why is that? Because your drive to achieve everything you desire will be infinite. Problems have solutions, your eyes are open to opportunities and you will never miss a chance to get where you want to. The belief that you are going to make your life matter will be constant and your ambition will have no limits.

Do whatever it takes!

Looking back at your dead dreams, don't you believe they are dead because you stopped following them?

I had a dream of being a singer when I was a teenager and my mum was the only that believed in me, even when I didn't. (told you she is the best)

She got me a teacher at the age of 13 and booked my first lesson in; I have done exactly what an unconfident teenager would do: rebelled. I cried and said 'no'. That got canceled because I wasn't considering myself good enough and not seeing myself being able to successfully sing. That dream died a long time ago because I didn't pursue it. My dreams changed as I moved through life and I have no regret for that particular thing as it taught me a great lesson: giving up means you failed.

Now that I know that, I am sure it will never happen again and each dream and goal I set for myself will be deeply thought of and laid out in front of me so I can see the benefits, value and how it enriches the people around me.

The trick on not giving up is seeing everything that comes in your way as the means to achieve your goals. You will encounter many challenges but the mindset shift is to see everything as becoming part of your journey, your growth and to make it even more desired and worth working for.

"What stands in the way, becomes the way"

I cannot say how important this is in achieving your dream life.

When you reach your destination, all the problems you faced become meaningless and you will thank yourself for not stopping the process you consciously started.

Even if you are at a crossroads and you feel overwhelmed, the power lays within yourself and the choice is yours: if you continue pursuing that dream or if it's not worth going through challenges for it.

For everything you encounter there is a solution, there is someone that knows more than you do, there is a book, a course, a new idea to undertake. So, quit the bs, stop being lazy and make your life better than it is, even if it is already fantastic.

There is a 3 step process to use whenever you set your desires. You probably heard about the 3 case scenarios for every situation. I like to do this with all my targets.

Every time you have to take decisions about your goals and your path, analyze what is the worst that can happen. Maybe is to lose some money, a job, wasted time, etc.

Any of these things can be achieved back, a job it's something you can have again, money is out there, the time it's something you cannot get back, but if you have a growth mindset you will see the benefits of having that time spent on the particular thing that you wanted.

So, now that we agree that the things you could lose in the 'worst' case scenario are easy to get back, we move on to the best part, the best-case scenario.

This case scenario has to thrill you, to inspire you and your life to be completely transformed by it. The situation that nearly seems impossible to achieve, but if you do get there, life will never be the same.

And last is the case that is most probable to happen. This is the middle way between the previous 2, which when achieved, will still feel worth the work you have been putting into it and you will still be satisfied with the outcome.

It is extremely important to look at this when you have tangible, rational goals that can be measured. Look at all 3 possibilities and focus on the best one; put your focus, energy and time into achieving the best-case scenario because even if it won't be exactly as planned, I guarantee you won't be disappointed. It is all about knowing what you want to achieve, having a high target, but also understanding that things could go wrong or have some unexpected challenges. That's why mindset is so important; because if that is in the right place you can guide yourself on getting back on track and keeping your focus on the goal. This is not wishful thinking and being positive, it is about keeping yourself on the right path and having a solution-focused mindset. Be ready for unexpected situations, but don't focus at all on them.

Another tip on goal setting is to make it about others. As much as you would want to be famous or successful in your own way, you should picture it in a way that will change your life and the life of those around you. When we want to get something because it helps others, we become even more in tune with the outcomes and we tend to work a bit more. We are not alone and we should all want to add value to others; the more we do for others, the more fulfilled we get. Having dreams that contribute to other people's lives makes all the struggle worth it.

That is one of the greatest things to remember, because it will influence everything around you, the way you see yourself, the way you see others, the ambition and determination; you have a higher motivator and now a purpose!

Stop being yourself!

Has being yourself brought in your life everything you desire? If yes, then you are on a great path and you don't need to read further.

If not, you understand my point of view. 'being yourself' is such a limiting statement. How many times did you hear people telling you 'just be yourself, things will turn around'-and they didn't.

That is because being just yourself is not enough. We are amazing human beings and we are enough, but that has nothing to do with these limitations everyone tries to impose on yourself and make you stick to your comfort zone.

This 'be yourself' statement that goes around it's a joke;

I say it "know yourself and adapt".

If you desire anything in life, it can be a job, a relationship, better health or anything else, you know you have to do certain things differently than the way you have been doing them.

You will have to learn new skills, change certain behaviors, evolve yourself in any kind of way, depending on your goals.

Don't believe that statement. Don't get comfortable with just who you are! You are enough and you are a whole package, but to constantly be yourself means no progress through life and excuses will start to appear.

It has a negative output and people that say this are doing it from a belief of 'just be yourself-things will fall from the sky'

Don't be yourself because you can be so much more than what you are!

Know yourself and adapt!

Stop using 'being yourself' as an excuse!

Self-image

You already have a self-image about yourself, what you need to do is look into that and see if that imagine you hold for yourself is a positive or negative one. Look into your qualities, defects, appearance and emotional state.

Everyone believes certain things about themselves, about their abilities, their looks, their achieving potential. Is it propelling you forward with your life or is it keeping you back? What is the image you hold for yourself? Based on psychology research we all have personalities inclined for happiness, unhappiness, success, failure, health or sickness. The personalities speak for themselves, what matters is, which one is predominant within yourself?

Based on that you can see the picture you have for yourself; if you are a happy person, if you believe people are out there to get you, if you believe and act like diseases are easily getting to you, if you believe you are meant to be successful in anything you desire to do or do you keep your goals low because you believe is not probable for you.

Know this about you, you were born to be extraordinary, not average, you were born without fear of failure and self-doubt, you were created confident and not fearful.

Figuring out what kind of image is the one you have been acting upon is no doubt one of the main things you want to do in order to live your life at its best.

Self-awareness

To have a strong and clear mind you to master your self-awareness. This is the basis of everything you will do in life if you want to achieve the successful life you are dreaming of.

Self-awareness is the keyword. Paying attention to your thoughts and feelings without judgment, but by analyzing everything that goes on inside of you.

The first thing that I have on my vision board (you should create one as well) is a command that I see from the moment I wake up and is this "reflect before reacting". Too many of us let ourselves be controlled, act and react emotionally before thinking things through, just to realize later on that we could have said things better, had a better approach or we end up even to regret certain things.

No matter the situation, we should always think before answering or doing something on an impulse. We should know already how we feel about certain subjects or certain people and we should control the way we behave and respond in those situations.

To move forward on the subject of self-awareness, as much as we need to pay attention to our thoughts, feelings, reactions, etc., we need to look into the things we don't want to pay attention to/ Whenever we don't want to think about certain things is because we are lying to ourselves when we find reasons for doing and saying things that we normally know we wouldn't do is because we are not true to ourselves. It comes easier for us to say "I don't want to think about that" than actually sit with ourselves and understand why certain subjects we let in the hands of 'fate'. I believe behind that, it's a very important survival mechanism that we don't pay attention to. It's the mind keeping you comfortable. As soon as you start analyzing your own self, paying attention to your thoughts and feelings, you see that some of them are not making a lot of sense or come from a darker side of you. When you realize that you can change, you become uncomfortable. So, in this case, your mind is telling you to stay the same, react, behave like you always did because otherwise if you find out things about yourself, you will have to change. If you find out that you have been saying, doing, reacting in a way that is not beneficial to you or those around you, you will be compelled to change. If you don't change, guilt comes over you. That is not a good feeling to have.

When you feel guilty, when you feel like you could've done things differently and you still don't do it, your conscience becomes heavy. Let's take an example like smoking. Everyone knows is not good for them, but do they like to hear it? Is anyone searching for the exact reasons why smoking is not good? Are people looking to do health checks to see how they get affected by smoking? Do they think about all of this? The vast majority doesn't, even though they know is not good and there are chances of creating sickness in their whole body. (I have been guilty of this myself)

So, basically, the chat goes something like this "yeah, I smoke. I know it's not good but I cannot stop cause I like it." This is one of the versions. Do you think that if any of these people will have a look into the health issues caused by smoking, properly research it, will still be happy to do it? They will probably do it, but the guilt feeling will be installed inside. And that is something that harms you mentally and physically. You can never say you know something and do the exact opposite. That is the reason we don't analyze ourselves and don't look deeper into different issues; the compelling fear of having to change something about the way we have behaving. So, the vast majority Is looking for things to numb their pain, for instant gratification, for anything that keeps them away from the 'real' pain. Change. And in that case, lying to ourselves comes in hand and superficiality takes over.

To continue with your perfect self, I would say that you need to create it beyond the norms of average, normal. You need to create this wonder woman that is achieving everything in her life. Your focus needs to change on what it's possible and what you can do, not on the current situation you're in, even it's an amazing one.

I am repeating this statement as I want to enforce the importance of this. Everyone that you admire and made a difference in the world knew some basic things: who they are, what they want and had a big dream aligned with their purpose. This is the reason why I say that again.

Don't forget to give yourself props for what you have accomplished so far and move on to what you can do next. We all have unlimited potential, hunger and drive, we just don't put it to its best use. Let's switch our thinking on what can we become and achieve, and not on the misfortunes around us.

Put your potential to work on positive matters, on creating a better future for yourself, on becoming a healthier, fitter, happier and more fulfilled version of you. Don't use all of that productive, creative energy on matters that harm others or yourself.

Believe with all your being that you can achieve it.

Daily, act upon it.

So, moving on self-chatter

Let's talk about the way you talk to yourself. Everyone has an inner chat at any given time of the day; I am having one right now, while I am writing this. The most important thing is to know if it's a negative or positive chat, if it brings you down or gets you lit up, if it contributes to your dreams or not.

The best way of seeing this is by taking an example, let's say you do some house cleaning. What is your mind preoccupied with while you do the actions that are kind of robotic? Or when in the gym, what is your mind telling you? Pay attention to the conversations that are happening in your mind, because they can show you something great if you just become present in that moment. The thoughts that we are daily having are 90% the same ones of the previous day, so you have a 10% chance of changing the way you are thinking. It may sound low, but every day to do this will rewrite all of your beliefs and get you in tune with who you really are.

How do you talk to yourself when you do something wrong or make a mistake? Are you saying something like "oh, you are so clumsy, you always get it wrong" Or are you saying "next time I will be more careful not to happen again"?

Get the difference between the two types of self-talk, one is making a statement that you are always doing something wrong, that you are a person that makes mistakes all the time and the other type of conversation is the fact that the particular mistake is a one time off and you learned your lesson and you are not repeating it next time; it also says that is not who you are, is not your character and it doesn't define you as a person.

It's the automatic response, the reaction to any given circumstance or experience, that is the self-talk. Make it a productive chat, a talk that benefits you, empowers you and becomes an example. Self-awareness is the best skill to master. The more self-aware you are, the better you know yourself, guide yourself and live up to your potential.

After you go through the first step, to identify the conversations you have with yourself, you will have to change the chatter by practicing conscious affirmations.Start telling yourself how amazing you are, how great you can be, how much you will influence others, how you are going to help the people around and how you are going to make a positive change in this world. Change your own life so you can help others change and improve theirs. It all starts with you.

"Everyone has inside of him a piece of good news. The good news is that you don't know how great you can be! How much you can love! What you can accomplish! And what your potential is!"

☐ *Anne Frank*

I believe it all starts with one person changing itself in order for others to crave a change. Just like I was thinking that I was the only one in my group of friends back in the day, that thinks things differently, I was always convinced that somewhere on this planet must be another person thinking in the exact same way and being concerned about the same matters things.

We want a different life than what society and community tells us we should have, we want to rise higher than what it was set for us and we can and we will.

Start your positive chat with yourself now, transform everything negative you already told yourself into an uplifting affirmation, don't let limitations get in your way and have the courage to do it; because you truly are amazing.

A different kind of self-talk is the mental chatter about yourself when you fail to do something, when you feel guilty, ashamed or not good enough. Be very careful because whatever you think about yourself is what you believe about yourself. And you want to be a whole package woman so that means the whole package woman is not silly, stupid, not worthy or not good enough. Put it this way, if you would have a child and you would hear "her" or "him" saying the things you are saying about yourself unconsciously like "oo I was so silly doing that" "I acted so stupid in that moment" "i am just not good enough" I believe you wouldn't appreciate it, actually you would be quite sad about the fact that the perfect child of yours can say such things. And if you have children, be careful about what you say around them because they are constantly learning from you, your words and your behavior.

As a final thought, becoming self-aware of yourself is one of the most important things to do. Pay attention to the thoughts that you are thinking, the feelings that come with those thoughts, the inner chatter you are having with yourself, the reactions that are happening automatically. It is known that 90%of the time, we are ruled by our subconscious, but allowing time to analyze and evaluate ourselves we can change the patterns that are controlling us.

Another mind chatter is the one in which we are having a mental conversation with someone else. Let's say there were some things left unsaid at today's meeting at work, or someone hurt your feelings and you didn't stand up for yourself or you wish you still had a chance to say some things to a person close to you or you simply think of a future conversation with someone else.

This is a waste of time. Truly!

I am going to give you a personal example of having a mental chatter with someone else. This situation happened one year ago.

I was at work having my food. I most of the time cook for myself since I am following a plant-based diet. I am having my food in small portions, more times a day, it gives me a boost of energy every time I have some. So, here I was, a 15-minute break, getting my salad, having it from the box, when suddenly I colleague (girl) comes in, puts a grin on her face and tells me "enjoy!". Do you know those kinds of smiles and head-nodding like someone means something else than what they say? She just gave me that. I answered "thank you! I am enjoying it." She then told me "I have noticed that lately, your belly is showing more". My answer to this affirmation was "interesting because my scale doesn't say that." And she said back "maybe you are just super bloated." Ladies, I admit; I was unprepared that in my 15 minutes break someone will tell me I was gaining weight. I had no answer to her last comment. If you know that emoji with the eyes popping out, that was me. I have just been called fat and I didn't respond to that. Guess what happened in the next week whilst I was driving every day to work? I was having a mental conversation with this girl. Being reasonable and respectful I believed, answering back to her calling me fat. Respectful and reasonable I said, I lied; I mentally roasted her in my mind.

I wasted so much time on all those thoughts and all that chatter that I could've used listening to my books or enjoying some music. I don't regret that because I have learned my lesson. I need to face people whenever someone tells me something with the intention to hurt me. It is as simple as that. You must be self-aware when your mind starts to wander away on things that don't matter.

There are 2 things that can be done when your mind is having a go at someone else. One of them is writing it down. It makes miracles, trust me. Let's say you're in an unexpected situation and you have no answer or you don't know how to react. A few minutes or hours later you find yourself thinking about it, replying to that person and spending too much time on it. I suggest writing all of that down, getting it out of your way and off your mind. Now, you put it somewhere and you are free to live your life and follow your dreams.

It may sound like a small thing to do, but just start paying attention to your thoughts and see how many times you think about something or someone without speaking up-it's crazy. That's the way this helps, it makes you release the emotions you have over that particular subject and frees your mind. Don't be afraid of the things you will write down, because you will experience a harsh part of yourself and a very opinionated one, but after you do it, you will also start to see a different side to the story. Life is not just white and black and things are not just good or bad.

If you want to take things even further, this would be the second thing you could do: having a conversation with that person. But it has to be a truthful one, no emotions involved and very calm and logical.

You could always avoid a confrontation like this and be settled with your own mind, but if you want to have a conversation about the subject in matter, you have to give up the black and white thinking and see beyond that person's words.

Why?

The best question to ask yourself is Why.

For absolutely everything you do in life, from food to marriage to a TV show, you have to ask yourself why.

Just picture yourself as a little kid that wants to know everything. It can be quite stressful because for many why questions we don't have an answer. Why is the fork called a fork? I don't know why, I just know that is a fork and that I need it.

But the why questions need to be approached on a deeper, self-discovery level.

Ask yourself every step of the way why you do or say certain things and don't be afraid of the answer. Face yourself. It will be quite hard in the beginning because you will tend to lie to yourself in order to keep that image we have been talking about. But you need to be straight forward with yourself and see the repetitive patterns in your thoughts.

Some examples of why questions and please answer them. You will see that the answer is not what you were expecting if you dwell and think about them long enough.

Why do you live where you live? Most of the people I know will say "because it's where I live" or "I lived there before and it's ok" or the one I keep hearing is "because it's close to work".

Now, I have a strong opinion about this because I don't believe we should choose where to live based on a job that most probably doesn't fulfill us. I think where we live should be a place that we like, that we enjoy spending our time around, love what we are surrounded by, maybe have friends and loved ones around and maybe after that, asses the distance between work a home.

Another why questions is for the job you're doing. Start to question everything around you, but mainly yourself.

So, why are you doing the job you are doing?

What is your reason for doing the job you're doing? To pay bills? Because you need money to survive? How many people actually answer that the reason is that they absolutely love it?

Ask yourself why, don't lie to yourself, don't find excuses and start changing the things you do 'just because', with things that you love and get you closer to your dreams.

The same question applies to your everyday life, from the choices you make with food, friends, relationships, job, career, hobbies.

For example, I personally choose to have a plant-based diet because I have been doing my research for the last few years I believe we are being sold a big lie about our nutrition. Do you know what you are eating and why you are eating those kinds of foods or you're doing it just because that's what you have been told since you were young? Find out what your body needs, find out how much nutrients, vitamins and food preferences you have and make a plan and stick to it. Mainly, find out why and question yourself and others.

Why are you in the relationship you are? Is it love? Is it just because you are used to it? If you are single, why are you single?

Don't give yourself bullshit lies about this, as we all know that "the quality of our relationships is the quality of our lives". Think about it for a while. Are you fully fulfilled or you just drag things along without facing the truth?

These WHY questions will take you far and deep; the most powerful one will be the ones where you question your own reactions. The way you talked to someone, the information you chose to share with a person, the way you behaved in a certain situation. When you look back and ask yourself "why did I say that" or "why did I behave that way" be true to yourself; don't blame anyone else as you are the only person in control of your feelings, words and actions. You might have done and said things out of sadness, suffering, jealousy or to hurt someone. The main point is to stop lying to ourselves; you don't need to share the answers with anyone and I recommend not to do it, but say it to yourself. You will become freer and you will see the lengths we go just to keep our own self-image.

Self-love and self-care is not self-ish

How do you know you are practicing self-love with yourself?
And how do you know what self-love is?

I have a very simple thought process in place when it comes to
this. For me, personally, self-love is prioritizing myself. My time.
It is the one thing we will never get back.

Self-love is being mindful of your happiness, mental state, building that relationship with yourself, listening to your own needs,
forgiving yourself and others because anything that makes you
feel bitter, sad, angry is not showing your true self the kind of
love it deserves.

Prove your love to yourself first.

I say that self-love comes on a spiritual and emotional level first.
You have to be mindful of your own needs, listen to your mind
and body. We may know what we want but the question to ask
ourselves is what we need. We know from our teacher Mr.
Tony Robbins that our values don't matter in the face of our
needs. That's why many of us still have habits that are unhealthy,
linger too long in unhappy relationships or are afraid to take
chances. Because that is the way we meet some of our needs.

Find out what your needs are in order to understand yourself,
allow yourself to enjoy whatever it is that you need, don't crit-
icize yourself and the main thing: knowing if your needs are beneficial to you or not. When you have needs of things that make
you unhealthy even though one of your values if health, you
need to work hard on changing it, otherwise, you will always be

in contradiction with yourself, judging and criticizing yourself.

Playing it on the rational level where you write down the good and the bad about the habits that fulfill your needs it's a very important step. You can asses how much good it does on your physical and mental health. All the habits can be destroyed and any habit can be built from scratch. Understanding the connection between your habits and your needs it's a must.

The needs, based on Tony Robbins are:

Certainty (being sure something brings you a certain feeling)

Uncertainty (the element of surprise)

Significance (being special)

Love and connection (speaks for itself)

Growth

Contribution

I will like to ask you to have a look at Tony Robbins's explanation of needs, as he is the best at talking about it.

After you understand the 2 main needs that rule your life, you can see your life, your decisions, your habits with different eyes because now you know more about yourself. You can also identify the driving needs in others, which will help you interact better with those around you.

Self-love is strongly related to the needs each person has, starting with you.

Self-love also requires action, requires you to be self-aware, know yourself and don't lie or cheat on yourself. You need to pay attention to your feelings and everything that is negative has to go, every memory that doesn't bring a smile on your face has to lose the power over you, every wrong you or someone else has done needs to be forgiven and forgotten. Practice self-love by forgiving yourself and those around you, let go of grudges, let go of expectations and just love yourself for who you are.

Your mental health is the best way to show yourself the love you hold inside for the amazing human being that you are. Prioritize your well being when it comes to the people around you, the time spent with things you don't necessarily love, show yourself the love and attention you wish to receive from others, buy yourself flowers, have a nice meal on your own. Celebrate being you!

I had a recent conversation with a friend and he told me I was getting selfish. The actual translation of being selfish is that one has no consideration of others and is self-centered. I explained to my friend that it is not the best word used to describe my attitude. I describe it as being in tune with my feelings and not letting outside negativity influence my inner peace. You are not being selfish if you don't want to hang around with people that bring negativity, gossips and start conflicts. You are not selfish if you prioritize your time and the activities you wish to do instead of focusing on other people's wants. You are not selfish if you are working harder on yourself and for yourself than for anyone else. You are not selfish for having dreams, setting goals and working to achieve the things you want in life.

Practice self-love and self-care by prioritizing yourself.

"Every man's happiness is his own re-sponsibility" A.Lincoln

What does it mean to be happy?

All of the great thinkers had a definition for happiness. We are no less than them, we have unlimited potential, so why not create our own definition of happiness. What does it mean to You?

My own definition of happiness is "enjoying the present moment".

Even more important than that, it is knowing happiness. By that, I mean recognizing when you are or were happy. The feelings you had, the thoughts you were processing, the environment you were part of and the people you were surrounded by. Based on my own definition of happiness that's the way I can identify the moments I am most happy in my life.

We control our happiness.

Do you remember the last time you were happy? If yes and it's more than a day ago, you are not living your life at its fullest. The last time you were happy should be yesterday because you made yesterday count and understood that we are not being promised tomorrow. Happiness it's an inside job that cannot be measured in materialistic items.

Is it your life worth living if you don't feel that emotion?

It would take a really dramatic event for me to let myself be overcome by negative feelings. The daily attitude is such a positive one that can be contagious and the everyday mindset is that everything and anything can be sorted, no matter what life throws at you.

The questions to ask yourself are: do you like to feel stressed, anxious, angry or upset?

Do you believe you can change the way you feel?

The answer to the last question should be "yes". A big fat one.

No one is in control of our feelings, but us. No one can make us focus on the negatives, but us. We are the only ones that can control where our attention and focus goes. Keep focusing on the things that can go wrong and you will never have peace. Keep focusing on what other people are doing and you will never have time to create your own life. It takes you the same amount of energy, focus and thoughts to think about the positives in any situation, as it takes to engage in wrongdoings and victimization. You are in control of your focus! You are the one that chooses!

Stop letting yourself be influenced by the things you cannot control and start managing the ones that only you can change.

Happiness comes from the moment we are not taking life for granted and we start being thankful for the little but big things in life. Just as normal as it may be to wake up in the morning and live another day, it's something we take for granted and don't even think about what we are getting. Just think about the importance of being here one more day; you get to enjoy the earth and what it has to offer, you get the chance to share the love with the people close to you, you have the opportunity to spend this day doing things that you enjoy.

Is it still such a little thing in life? It is probably the most important moment, to be here, to be present and to see the beauty in it.

Gratitude plays the most important role in happiness. Start your day by being grateful for getting another chance to be better, do better, enjoy, love and laugh. Make today matter. One thing is for sure, you can't feel misery when you are being grateful. Whatever you are being grateful for, expands, puts a smile on your face and makes your life meaningful because you don't take it for granted anymore.

Gratitude stands at the root of all happiness!

Everyone has been hearing others saying that you have to be grateful and that you have to practice it every day in the morning, but people mostly don't do it because they don't know how that it benefits their life and because their mindset is mostly set on "things happen to me"

Do you think you really understand what it means to be grateful? Do you actively think about being grateful? There is where the power is!

Are you grateful for being alive? For living each day? Do you understand you didn't have to do anything for your heart to keep beating?

That's the way you start seeing the importance of it.

Gratitude is not just a fancy word to make ourselves feel better because we know it and because we are suggested to try it. Gratitude comes from deep down, from understanding the importance of your life and from seeing how fortunate we already are.

If you want to improve your life straight away, start by dwelling a while on this. You are not here, on this earth just by chance, you matter and everything around you mustn't be taken for granted.

Be thankful for who you are today, what you have and where you are; and look forward to tomorrow to find new things to be grateful for, discover even more beauty and unleash your powers.

Being grateful doesn't mean you settle for what is set out for you; it means you can see all the positives of being here right now. Use that wisely.

The next level of gratitude is when you are grateful for something that didn't go your way. This one is a tough one, that I have been struggling with aswell. Can you really be grateful for being laid off or breaking up with someone? Yes, you can! you hold the power of changing that and see all the benefits that come from something being perceived as negative. Being grateful for unexpected, sad events that might occur says a lot about you and about the direction you are heading towards. You can change everything from a negative to a positive, just by understanding the value, knowledge and experience it comes with it.

I challenge you again by looking at a past event that had a 'negative' outlook, perceived by the majority, and really, deeply thinking about everything that brought in your life afterward. Open your eyes to see the good outcomes, the experience, the learning lessons, the possibility of something new and master the gratitude idea.

Be grateful for the happy moments and for the ones that made you feel less good in the past. The more you focus on the happy moments you experienced, the more will come your way. It's a fact! When it comes to the less fortunate moments in your life, make sure you are grateful for those as well because they teach you a lesson, even if you see it or not. Take a relationship as an example: you might not feel so good about having it ended, but by focusing on all the times you enjoyed yourself being in there with your significant other, changes your attitude towards what happened in the past and sets you on a path of success in the future. It also makes you feel appreciation, don't hold grudges and expect better things in your life. If you could feel that good in a relationship that didn't work in the long run, can you picture how amazing it would be a relationship that both of you share the same values and love each other?

Make sure you learn the lessons that each experience brings you, analyze yourself, find out what your needs and values are, get to know yourself better and look at people with a deeper, more insightful understanding.

I grew up in a place where the word happiness was not mentioned, mainly because people were more focused on survival. It took me years in my adulthood to see and feel the moments that I enjoyed with my all being. I started realizing what happiness feels like at the age of 23 when I became aware of the gift that life is.

What is life to you? Is it a constant chase for the next best thing, a fight for survival, a competition with others?

Be aware of the way you live your life, your daily routine and your belief about the meaning of it. Do you believe you have a purpose? Because you do! Everyone has one and everyone has their value to bring to others and this world.

Life is about being and doing your best, adding value to the people around you and last but not least, enjoying every single day.

We must accept the things we cannot control

We all know that emotions are being categorized into 2 big departments. We all have negative and positive emotions. We can feel love, joy, playfulness, excitement and we can feel frustration, anger, disgust and fear. These emotions are feelings that change our physical and psychological state and influence our behavior.

A negative one will make us act in a negative manner, whilst a positive emotion will have a positive result.

Our lives are being ruled by our emotions; the people we chose around us, the things we buy, how we spend our time and the way we interact with others. Emotions are a big part of our decision-making process. We want to live our lives in a healthy emotional awareness.

In order to control the way we respond or act in certain circumstances, we need to pay close attention to the way we feel. This is the first step of identifying your own emotions and taking control of yourself. Know that if you're in a good mood, everything around you will seem nice, warm, kind; but if your own mood is not that good and you are experiencing some kind of negative emotions, your whole perception about the things around you will change into a negative one.

Listen to your thoughts, feel your energy inside you and how it manifests, see your body's reactions to the feelings you are experiencing and label that exact state.

Know how you are feeling at any time!

After you know the state of your own mood, you need to know that you can change it. You can really stop feeling like shit! Honestly! You can!

You can wake up on the wrong side of the bed or feeling alone or thinking that you gained weight (assuming it's a negative thing), you can experience any type of negative emotion and it's only you that can change how you are feeling about it.

You have to pay attention to the things and actions that boost your mood and if you don't know which one are those, you will have to figure them out because they will be your state savior. The most common things that make us feel good are cheering music, talking to a friend (we all know we love that), having time on our own where we do something special, going for a walk, do some shopping, meditate and the list goes on. There are plenty of activities that uplift our mood- it just depends on each person's preferences.

I, love all of the ones mentioned above and I don't necessarily need to engage in any of them to feel better at any given point because I have learned during many years how to shift my focus and change my thoughts from negative to positive. This is where you will get by following step by step what I have been telling you from the beginning. It took me years of working on myself, to understand and practice how I can shift my emotions, but it's a never-ending journey and the more you do it, the better you become at it.

During the last few years, I realized how important is for me, my state, the way I feel. It should be the same for everyone. There is nothing more important than the way you feel. The challenge for our emotional state is when negative events occur and the way we deal with them. It may sound silly, but no one likes to feel angry, upset, frustrated, etc., and the beauty is that we can change that. This is not just a talk about seeing the good in everything, because there are events in life that challenge our perception and the switch to start having positive feelings can be harder to find.

It is about seeing the truth, seeing life as it is, with good and bad, but not focusing on the bad and wishing for better with every challenge we get. In the end, all the events and bumps in the road we get, they come up just for us to be able to identify better what we want and how would we be truly fulfilled. They are a blessing in disguise because they work for us to make it clearer there is a contradiction in what we actually want out of life.

Turn reactions into reflection

You need to master your reactions. To say it even better, you need to make your own emotions work for you not against you.

This is more focused on the negative states we get in when something goes wrong or unexpected around us. We tend to shout, cry, panic, behave in a way we normally wouldn't because we are not in control of ourselves. When you behave/ react in a way that is 'not you' that means you are not rational and in control of yourself.

We are not robots and we have feelings, but it's up to us if we are going to make a bad 'memorable' moment or day or if we choose to think first, and act after we are in a neutral state.

We need to express our feelings but the way we do it says a lot about us. Stop ranting, complaining, judging and think before you speak. Think twice about the message you are about to get across and WHY you feel the way you feel. We already know the importance of why and the best scenarios to apply it to is when you are emotional. Why are you feeling frustrated about that certain event? Why is that particular thing making you angry? Why are you feeling stressed when you have to do a certain thing? Ask yourself why all the time and you will understand yourself so much better.

Reflect before you react because no one likes to say things they don't mean in a moment of emotional turbulence. Reflect because you don't want to apologize for something you said or done because you were not in control of yourself. Reflect because you get a better understanding of yourself and others. Reflect because you will never regret anything in your life, said or done.

Be the Non-Drama woman

That is a whole package woman, a woman that doesn't engage in any drama and doesn't allow anything toxic to come in her life. A woman that is calm, happy, that people like having her around, that brings a sense of peace and control. Distance yourself from gossips, judgments, complaints, comparisons and all the rest. If at the current moment people are coming to you to tell you the latest gossip, I am sorry to say but you are engaging in too much drama. You are not being a whole package woman.

Don't allow such insignificant things and behaviors to take the best of you and transform into this woman that always has something happening to her or always has some news about others to spread around. Don't be that.

People don't like those kinds of people around them, even better said, the people you want in your life don't concern themselves with such matters. Don't be the reason people get stressed, worried or nervous when you are around. Change that into receiving a smile any time you meet someone because they know how kind, warm and calm you are. Bring joy to others and let your presence be enjoyed by everyone. Leave a good taste to people's mouths.

Encourage growth and positivity; teach others how to support each other; share love and compassion; engage in constructive activities and conversations; appreciate the value others are bringing into your life;

This is how we create more whole package women!

We have been talking about finding out more about yourself, identifying feelings, behaviors, beliefs and so on. We, now, know how to challenge our beliefs, how to aim higher in life and why; we know how to identify our emotions and change our state of mind; we have a clearer picture of what has been holding us back.

This is great and this kind of personal work has to be done continuously as we change and as don't want to just "be ourselves".

The next step is figuring out what we want and what our dreams are. Many of you already got some picture in their minds of what exactly you want to achieve in life.

There are many exercises in order to identify those wild and hidden passions. There is no more time to waste, no more time available to just throw it out the window on insignificant matters.

Life is happening today and now and you need to do things that make your heart sing.

As I broke down the book in 5 chapters, we have been working on the first one, but just to get an empty mind to see the things you desire and to stop limiting yourself.

The next 4 chapters are about spirituality, health, relationships and wealth.

To identify your true desires you need to do start envisioning yourself at your best, to start picturing your perfect day and your perfect week. Start thinking about the things you would do and how you would spend your time.

Read and answer the following questions:

How would you look like at your best?

What would you do every day if you would have back your time?

How much money would you want per month?

Do you have a dream car or home in mind? Or both?

Where would you live?

How would you spend your time with your friends?

How would your life partner be like?

Where would you travel?

How would you give back to your community?

How would you contribute to helping others?

The aim of these questions is to start dreaming, to start seeing how achievable is everything. All the answers to the questions above are real, other ordinary people achieved them, so there is no potential limit unless you set one.

Chapter III

Spirituality

This is the key step in following through with your life vision. This is what it will make you stay on track and keep you in tune with your desires.

First of all, you will have to spend time on your own and think about your biggest dreams in as many details as possible. Have that clear image of your perfect self.

Second, you will be creating a list of all the things you want to achieve and place it somewhere where you can see it every day.

Third, affirm everything you wish to accomplish as you have already done.

Feel it through your whole body.

This undeniably will keep your focus on yourself. You won't have time to gossip about others, you won't engage in negative situations, you won't be bothered by other people's opinions and it will make you act upon your dreams.

When you lose your vision, your attention from yourself, your energy is being used in other unproductive mental and physical activities. You shouldn't care about the way others chose to live their life, about what others are doing with their time, or how are they doing in their job, unless you can help in any way to improve.

After you decide on what you want, you need to practice your affirmations and visualize it every day. When you don't do that, you are no longer at your best. Like I said in the beginning, we already are whole package women and that comes to fruition by every day striving to be and do better than the day before.

The moment you are not in tune with your desires, with the

things that make your heart sing, you are losing your momentum and your crave for life.

The spiritual aspect of life has been neglected by many people, mainly because they believe it's associated with religion. Being spiritual means having that inner peace, being connected to something bigger than yourself, either found in nature, religion, art, universe; it's about finding that purpose of life, living your life with a meaning and it's usually something unseen to the eyes of people but felt within your soul.

I would say that meditation can bring you closer to what your own definition of spirituality is, there is no right or wrong, as different things and practices can make us feel connected to our inner self.

Meditation nowadays is a practice known by many people and some are doing it on a daily basis. I will be covering 3 types of meditation that I practiced but I can say that there is no one thing for everyone and these are the ones I have tried and now I am moving forward only with one of them as it suits me better.

Mindfulness is the most common form of meditation and it requires 10 minutes of your time where you count until 10 all that time. Inhaling on your nose, exhaling on your mouth and acknowledging the thoughts that are coming in your mind, but keep on counting. Every time you realize you stopped counting and start thinking, you start again from 1.

There are apps you can download that guide through the whole process (headspace and calm) are the most used ones.

I recommend getting one of them and start doing it every day because the benefits of having and maintaining that inner peace is priceless. Every great person that achieved some kind of success has been practicing a form or another of meditation.

Look into it.

Another form of meditation is the transcendental mediation that I was introduced to by a close friend. I can say that I didn't practice it for a long time as I started doing metta meditation. Otherwise, I would've continued with TM. In TM you sit down twice a day for 20 minutes and you go into this process. You will find yourself a word without a meaning, invented one and for 20 minutes you keep saying it, out loud preferably (not shouting ofc)

What this helps you achieve is not thinking about the usual things you would probably do because the word has no meaning to you and constantly saying it won't allow you to focus on the basic stuff you would do. You can even come up with great ideas during this type of meditation. Try it!

And my favorite

Metta meditation.

I wish I would knew about this earlier. It's been amazing for me. In metta meditation, you would normally say 3 words for 20 minutes. Like "love, kindness, gratitude"; personally I prefer to adapt the words based on my day and how I feel. Before starting mediation I would place my hand on my heart and ask "what do I need today?" , "what does my heart want to know?" (something I have learned from a great lady in Marbella) and after that, listening to myself and being aware of my emotions, I would start meditating with exactly what I need for the day. (feelings expressed in words)

At the moment it's my favorite kind of meditating as I can change it every day, it's never boring, makes me aware of myself and it feels great afterward.

Affirmations and visualisation

I personally put these two things together as you can not do one without the other. Even if you would, the effect and power of it wouldn't be the same.

I love visualizing everything I desire in my life and I set my intentions by doing the affirmation work. After you set your goals, whatever they are, start visualizing each one of them with your eyes closed and see yourself as you have already got it. Let's say you desire a specific kind of car, close your eyes and see it, feel it, drive it, picture everywhere you would go, who you would be taking with you, what kind of music you would listen to and so on. Alongside that start saying your affirmation regarding this particular intention. All my affirmations are starting in this way "I am so happy and grateful for". So in this example, it would go like this "I am so happy and grateful for having this car". You realistically don't have it, but you need to get used to saying it and believing that you are going to get. Feel everything about getting that car, all the emotions and the excitement that comes with achieving this goal.

I have affirmations for every area in my life, more than one for some of them and for each affirmation I have set a time to achieve it "by March 2020" for example in the car scenario above.

I did achieve many things in my life through affirmation and visualization and it's not like things fell from the sky, but the intention and the daily focus to achieve my goals was there because every day I was engaging in the process I am talking about.

Don't underestimate the power of thoughts and also remember that this is the way the subconscious gets overruled, by repeating things constantly that will either help you grow or will keep you down, comfortable. It is your choice to control your thoughts, (kind of cliché to say that) your intentions and your focus.

For a month I have been doing my affirmations in a notebook and visualizing it every time I was writing it down. Also, saying it out loud whilst doing that.

After a month I got into the habit of doing it and now every time I am in the car and I am driving I will automatically say my affirmations.

Something else that helps is recording yourself and play those affirmations to yourself.

It is so powerful this kind of work that until you do it, you won't see the benefits. Your mind won't wander at irrelevant issues that occur in your daily life and it will help you make better choices in regards to your future and in accordance with goals.

I read a book a few months back that was talking about the importance of words and how different words make us feel different things, from one person to another. So, I made a list of all the important words that I felt were producing a positive emotional reaction in my body. It is not a long list but I introduced those words into my daily affirmations and it makes miracles. For example when I was saying 'influence' I didn't really feel it, but when I say 'inspire' it just lightens me up. That is one word I consciously changed in my daily routine just to keep me emotionally involved with all my goals.

You can do it to.

Write that list with words that have an impact on you, write down the intentions you have for yourself like you already achieved it "I am so happy and grateful" (that works for me, but for you could be different wording) and say it out loud while picturing you already got it.

Sounds simple but it will be a mental battle at the beginning with your monkey mind that will try to constantly remind you that you didn't achieve those dreams, that's why you need to train it to work for you and with you, to get closer and closer day by day to your desires.

Vision board

A picture is worth a thousand words.

. Having that vision board with the things you are working for and see it every day just enhances the work you have previously done. Make sure everything you set on that board is in tune with yourself and also, make sure that they are your dreams and not someone else's.

Feel free to add everything there, no judgment; look at it every day. You will find yourself getting used to it and not really getting into that state everytime you see it, but our brains are working on two important things: repetitions of words and pictures. And when your brain sees every day the same pictures it will inevitably push you closer to what resembles that. Make your mind your friend, make it work for you, train is and tame it, otherwise, it won't set you up for success.

Chapter IV

Health

Let's move on to another subject which is the physical part of ourselves.

As a whole package woman, the body you are living in is the main visual point.

How do you celebrate your working body? Are you grateful for the health that you are in? Do you take time daily to do something to keep its vitality? Or do you take it for granted and remember that it needs care once in a blue moon?

We are women, we are aging, we carry babies, we have periods. Basically, our bodies are most of the time under stress. Diet, sleep, exercise and relaxation is what it needs.

Your beauty comes from inside and we all know that, but the way we feel inside shows on the outside and vice versa.

Love your body first and it will show on the outside. Take time to be grateful for its mechanisms and for not giving up on you. It's a part of you that requires love and attention. You wouldn't be complete or whole without a good attitude and good care towards your physical part of you.

The best exercise I have ever done for my self-confidence, was talking to myself in the mirror. Many people avoid mirrors because it shows YOU, with your flaws and your own personal, physical characteristics. Look in that mirror and see yourself, your true self, the beauty that doesn't have to wear makeup, the kindness that your smile shows, the curves that show your femininity and all the marks that show your body's evolution. Love every inch of it. Promote amongst our own kind the self-love, respect and admiration for our bodies.

Go into that mirror and tell yourself how much you love yourself, how perfect your love handles are and how cute those thighs look. Everyday!

Did you know that people with eating disorders (anorexics, bulimics) are doing the opposite to be able to treat their bodies in a disrespectful manner? We have been born with no self-esteem issues, nor with self hate for our bodies. We were born perfect and love was impregnated in our genes; love for the self and love for others.

To be able to dislike ourselves we had to learn it and practicing it. One of the ways the people with eating disorders are doing that is by starting out looking in the mirror and tell themselves horrible things about their own looks. Isn't that cruel? What state of mind is that putting you into? Is it worth it, that in one life that we live on this earth, to hate ourselves and body shame ourselves?

I believe every woman went through a phase where they didn't feel like they were looking at their best, or that they could lose weight or change something about their own bodies. That's why, I want to make this a call out to all of you that know how that feels and help others that you see that are putting themselves down, especially teens. We wouldn't even consider those changes or analyzing every inch of our own bodies if we wouldn't compare ourselves with others, or listen to irresponsible famous people. Please, be aware of the message you send about the body image, self-love and physical appearance. You matter-you can influence! Make positive statements and share the love!

Practice the positive affirmations about your body in the mirror every day. Not only you will change your state of mind and mood, but you will also consider different options and choices, being focused on your own health. Don't change the nature of our humanity by unlearning how to love ourselves; you are still that perfect baby that has so much love to offer to yourself and others.

"I love every bit of my own body"

"I am so happy and grateful for my body weight, shape, skin colour and looks."

Start with yourself and spread it across.

Loving yourself with flaws and imperfections it's a sign of maturity.

Harsh truth: You will never be perfect!!

Accept yourself, love every bit of you because you're unique and that is your power. No one can take that away from you and it's the best way to build your confidence. This is not about getting complacent, this is about accepting the fact that you will never be perfect and accepting yourself and your body. Trust in that and also know that you are the only one that can change anything about yourself, but only do it from a place of gratitude.

Be grateful for your own body because it's the body you have achieved so much in life with, treat it with respect and nourish it in the best ways possible.

Focus on your health, well being, positive self-talk and improvements.

We all know that diet it's the way we nourish our bodies, the foods we eat are creating good health or poor health. Knowing how to choose what gives you energy and fulfills you is key in keeping it alive and lively. Personally, I have a plant-based diet in place because of the way I get my energy. I never feel sluggish or sleepy after eating a meal, it's exactly the opposite. I listen to my body and I see the effects of the foods I have been choosing to eat in the last few years. It truly is one of the best decisions I have ever taken to change my diet.

Diet is not a temporary change of eating habits, it's a lifestyle change.

The process when choosing the kind of foods you should eat should be as simple as this concept: "if you know where it comes from and how it's made, eat it".

If you have no idea of the processes that have been happening to your food before feeding it to your whole body, I recommend not to have it. I am not trying to convince any person to go on a plant-based diet, because most people "couldn't do it" but every dietician or nutritionist would tell you not to eat processed foods because of the hormones, chemicals and other added agents that will make you sick in the long run.

Be wise when it comes to nutrition, give your body what it needs and rarely what it wants. We may not want broccoli, asparagus and kale with every meal and it's okay to have a treat, but make sure that treat doesn't become a habit or a reason to have it for every win in your life. Don't find excuses to have cheat meals, introduce the cheat meals in your plan from the beginning, so that particular thing you will be eating is not a cheat, it's a reward for doing so many days of clean eating.

"We don't die, we kill ourselves"

I love this quote because it tells the truth when it comes to the lifestyles we are living. Just think about it; we know what causes us harm, what makes us unhealthy, what creates disease in our bodies and still do certain things. We don't die of disease and illness, we create those sicknesses because we make poor choices when it comes to health. It is as simple as that. All the information that we need in order to be healthy and live longer is out there as a form of studies, research, naturopaths and hundreds of years of knowledge. Why are we still suffering from cancer and many other diseases? Because we have been living our lives taking our health for granted. In the last 20 years, we had at least 30 new diseases occurring among us and they spread in different parts of the world. So, there are also new diseases coming out. It seems like we are progressing on some many different fields and areas and somehow we don't make any progress on our health and well-being. Technology, entrepreneurship, social media, online businesses, we all want the new best thing, but we forget the basics. We cannot enjoy any of it, if we lack health. As a homework, every time you are prone to making a decision about your lifestyle and health, think twice and ask yourself if there is a better option for the next move you are going to take. This is obviously if you want to live longer and have a better quality of life. We are in control of our health and our lifestyle. Illnesses don't just happen; they are a series of bad decisions that we make for a long period of time. If we can make those decisions that bring us misery, pain, obesity and damaging our health, we can also shift our mind to focus on health and wellbeing. We must be aware of what causes us harm and eliminate it from our lives.

Better choices, better lifestyle.

Another very important part when it comes to your health and your overall look is sleep.

Sleep is the nutrition of the brain.

During sleep our body is regenerating itself, clears out the toxins, repairing itself and restoring the hormones to normal levels. Sleep is needed for our normal nervous function and for the proper functioning of our organs. During sleep our mind takes a break from the most know function of flight fight, the muscles are on a temporary pause, the organs also slow down for us, etc.

The amount of sleep needed varies depending on the age of a person, but an adult needs about 7-9 hours of sleep.

I love sleeping and I am very grateful for the fact that I am able to benefit from a good night rest. As a person that used to work night shifts, the lack of nighttime sleep affected me and my overall health. I was craving for a routine, for a good night rest and it was very difficult to get a solid 8 consistent hours of sleep.

I struggled with my sleep for a long period of time, I have even been diagnosed with fatigue because of the little, inconsistent sleep I used to get. I am extremely grateful to say that now my life has changed and I am sleeping as much as I need to, during night time.

It's a fact that lost sleep will never be recuperated, so think twice before you do the "sleep faster technique"

The lack of sleep also makes you gain weight! The fogginess the brain is in when it's not rested pushes you to make bad choices. Also, it deals with a number of important hormones in your body that don't perform as well as they should because of the tiredness level. In a nutshell, sleeping doesn't make you lose weight, but the lack of it, makes you store more fat and make poor food choices.

When it comes to getting a good night's rest some of my tips are: don't eat or exercise before going to bed, try your best to stay away from blue light screens and read a book. This way you can catch up on your reading and also get relaxed and ready to fall asleep.

I love to sleep, it's such a great way to relax and recharge. I love siestas and napping aswell. The more I rest, the fewer eye bags and dark circles products I use.

That should be enough to convince you to get your sleep right and prioritize that rest time as never before. Phone off, light off, right temperature, positive thoughts. The energy you have when falling asleep, it's the same one that you will wake up in, so, make the next day a great day.

"Up in the gym just working on my fitness
He's my witness"

That's a song I seriously like, super energetic, gets you in the mood for working out and it's girly with a video full of fit women.

The mindset shift when it comes to working out is by doing it because you love it, not because you hate different it.

we need to love our bodies, but we need to love them in a way where we understand that each food choice and each exercise routine is going to have an impact on it. Exercising can be fun, exercising doesn't need to be done alone if you don't want to, exercising can be done in the comfort of your home or attending your gym, you have no excuses not to work your body out 30 minutes a day. Just like understanding that you need to take the dog for a walk, we need to understand that our bodies need daily movement aswell. If you have a car and you keep it in the driveway, you know for sure that it's going to get rusty and in time it will get old and break down. The same it happens with our bodies, we need to increase our heartbeats, we need to sweat, we need to work out all of our muscles, we need to start caring for our own health. Find your motivation when it comes to exercising, it may be some dress or a pair of jeans that it's been years since you didn't wear and get motivated to fit into it again, or it may be the fact that you crave for a better and longer life to be able to spend it with your (future) children and grandchildren.

I always prefer to have a deeper motivator, to have a high goal when it comes to anything but especially exercising and I push and I will always do it with everyone around me because we have been born to thrive not to survive. Live a long and healthy life!

A 30-60 minute time to exercise it's enough to do per day if you want to keep your shape, tone your muscles, get more energy, feel better about yourself and get leaner. A once or twice per week it's not going to produce a miracle, but 30 minutes daily or exercise routine will do. Work out for your health, for your personal image, for feeling better and more energised, but if you work out because YOU decided you would like to lose some weight, you will have to be a little bit more strict in the first couple of months. You can introduce your exercise routine at any time of the day, but the best results you will have early in the morning on an empty stomach according to myself and the Journal of Physiology. They also found out that working out between 1 and 4 pm also advances the body clock. In the end, it's down to you and when you plan it in your daily routine; it's important to have it in your schedule in order to follow through.

Myself, a couple of years ago, because of little free time during the day, I was exercising while cooking. So my 2 activities were something like this. Chop a carrot, 10 pushups, chop an onion 15 squats, peel potatoes 15 jumping jacks. Of course, all of them were being done in sets of 3 and 4, in order to keep my muscles in shape.

It also comes down to what you like as exercise. You may be into running, swimming, classes, home workouts, HIIT, yoga, dancing or many other different ways of moving your body. I personally love boxing and kickboxing. I also love, bodyweight training and home workouts because I fit them better in my schedule.

If you don't know what you prefer in matters of exercising, just go and attend free trials, get a free session with a personal trainer, go out there and try different things in order to see for yourself which one is more you.

One HIIT exercise I would like to recommend is Tabata; this is more for the ones that don't have time for walks in the park and attend 1-hour classes. The program works on a 4-minute exercise routine and it really works you out. It goes something like this. You pick 4 exercises that are working out the main muscles of your body or more exercises and you practice each one of them for 4 minutes. You do 20 seconds of the exercise and 10 seconds rest, this gets repeated 8 times in which you will reach the 4-minute exercise and then you move to the next one. You do as many different exercises as you wish and can, depending on your stamina and physical condition, but this one will make you work your body out.

"There is always time for squats"

I came up with this thinking about how much I would love a nice round bum just like all of the girls we see on Instagram posing and showing their glutes. Do you want it? You can have it! Squats is something I do quite often; even if I am not where I would like to be, bum fitness-wise, there is definitely progress. It doesn't even take long to do a few series of squats.

It's all about which part of your body you want to work out the most and change that quote to "push-ups", "sit-ups", etc. start taking action because the sooner you start, the sooner you will see results. Nothing happens overnight when it comes to being fit, it's the consistency that matters but when you look at your goals and remind yourself why you are striving for these things for yourself, you become an inspiration, a success story and a motivator.

I just want to remind everyone that I am not a dietician, nor a personal trainer; I am sharing results I had myself and others around me; as much as all of this is about routine and action, in the end, it's still the mindset that determines the results.

That being said, the most important thing is to remember that taking care of our bodies in all these ways must come from a loving feeling and not a hateful, disgraced or unhappy one.

Exercise, follow a healthier diet, sleep better, learn how to unwind because you love your body and not because you hate different aspects of it.

The next question for you ladies is how do you relax?

This is as important as everything else because we need to give our bodies a break; that's why we should introduce a treat meal in our weekly eating routine, we should also have a rest day from training and we should do something relaxing for our bodies

There are different ways to do that, depending on your time, budget, etc. A few hours on the weekend in a spa sounds great, getting a massage, sauna, pool, jacuzzi. We should make time for this, but many of us don't find a few hours a week to do that, so what if you create a spa at your place? I absolutely love baths, long bubble baths and that is my way of unwinding. What if you would do this weekly? Every Friday or Sunday or any other day of the week you prepare for yourself a nice warm bath, scented candles, the music that you love or a good book and just relax for an hour. I can already picture myself in the bathtub with a glass of wine as well.

There are different ways to relax physically and mentally, this is my way of checking both through one activity.

There are many other ways to get relaxed; by having a walk in the park, going for a manicure, read a book, have a coffee on your own, do something just for you and no one else. Basically, it's about giving yourself a rest, a break from everything you do on a daily basis, have an hour where the only thing you care about is 'chilling'.

Beauty is a genuine smile on anyone's face.

I have been thinking about giving an answer to a question lately, that I am going to ask you as well. What does it mean to be beautiful? What is beauty?

I believe beauty comes from inside and everyone that wears a smile on their face becomes beautiful. Beauty is subjective, what is looks beautiful to you, it might not seem the same to the person next to you. It's just the same with food preferences, style, attraction and all in between because we see beauty with our own unique perspective. There is no criteria to decide worldwide who is beautiful and who is not and I believe that is that way because everyone is beautiful by being unique. The charts with the most beautiful women or most attractive celebrities are being selected by popularity, not by deciding on certain features that a woman has to have. We can not live our lives believing that the top of the charts are the most attractive women everywhere and whatever is not similar to that is ugly or unattractive. Those tops are changing every year, so changing yourself to fit a chart like that is just not sustainable.

Think about the models for a bit, they need to have certain body dimensions in order to perform well in their careers, just like each one of us has to have certain skills to do our jobs or work in our business. Having those body criterias doesn't define beauty, it says the requirements needed for doing that job.

Beauty has nothing to do with body size or physical dimensions, so transforming our body and face to fit a specific woman type is not a healthy way of feeling beautiful.

I believe saying things like "it's not beautiful" or "that doesn't taste good" or "that haircut is terrible" is a wrong way of saying things. Your own perception is making those decisions based on your personal view, without taking into consideration other people's taste and preferences. I think we should change that to a more understanding and approving way of communicating, like " I wouldn't wear that myself since it's not my style" or "I, personally don't like cabbage" or "based on what I like, I believe she is really pretty".

Learn how to communicate in a way that you express your preferences and you don't offend or judge someone else. Just like life is not just black and white, beauty being part of it will be treated with the same principle. There is no universal ugly and no universal beautiful, it is all up to our own view in matters of this subject.

Self-care physically is a completely different matter than self care emotionally and mentally.

As much as you need to take care of the inner self, you need to look after your looks and appearance, as a whole package woman. I am talking about skin, hair, nails, clothing. I am talking about the first impression. What would someone think of you the first time they see you without any conversation? Do you think you neglect your looks? If you do, why do you neglect your appearance? Do you believe you do your best to feel and look good? Self-confidence and feeling beautiful comes from inside, but are you showing it outside? What is your belief about looking attractive?

The whole package woman invests time in her looks. It is all about the basics of the looks; your skin, your hair, your paws and claws, your outfit. We all experienced that one time we have to go to the grocery store and we don't want to put any effort into what we look like; and guess what? That's the moment we actually bump into someone and we wish we had done it different. Be ready for anything. Be ready for a spa day or a night out or a fancy dinner or jog in the park.

"You don't have to look like on the red carpet, to feel ready for the red carpet"

Make time once a week to take care of these areas of your body. You already know the confidence that gives you once you are on point with everything, So why not do it on a regular basis? Book that pedicure in, shave those legs, take the makeup off after a long day, buy that lingerie.

Just like beauty comes from inside, physical confidence comes from the lingerie.

It's the underneath that matters, gives you confidence and makes you feel attractive. Spending money on underwear and lingerie it's an investment for boosting your own self-confidence. You don't have to share that with anyone, just admiring yourself in the mirror will do its job; knowing how good you look and how attractive you are.

Did you notice how your mood changes every time you do a nice hairstyle or wear a piece of clothing that suits you well? I am not saying spend all your money on clothing, I am saying that you should take care of the things that make you feel good about yourself. Beauty comes from inside,but being comfortable in your own skin it's an outside job. You have to master the basics, be ready for anything and do more of what makes you walk with your head high and put your strong foot down.

Sexuality

I have been dwelling a lot on this subject since I didn't know if I should write anything about it now or leave it for another time (or age lol)

For many people, this is a sensitive subject that they tend not to discuss or they do it only in private with the ones they really trust. It can be controversial because of our beliefs and the culture we have been growing up in.

Since most of us are being raised with a fear of judgment, I have been thinking about many ways how to send my message across and I chose to share some important matters and act as an example of communication about this 'taboo' subject.

It is true that we are evolving and we are changing our mindset, but unfortunately, there are still many places in the world that sex and sexuality it is considered a sin and or something we shouldn't talk about freely.

Sexuality is a vast word that covers a big part of your personality.

I want to define it as an intimate preference that doesn't involve only sex and it defines you as a powerful gender. Sexuality is more of an energy that you transmit wherever you are. See it as an invisible force that is within us and guides throughout the day and in the way we act and interact with others.

You can just look at people and you can tell what kind of sexual energy they have; you can see if someone is a dominator, a submissive, hungry for some or having a good sexual life.

Your sexuality it's written all over your face and body whether you embrace it, block it, enjoying it or denying it. It is seen in the way you move, the way you stand, the way you talk, the way you smile. Your sexual energy it's being felt by people around you, you transmit it whenever and wherever you are by being physically present in any environment.

What is it that you like, who do you prefer as a partner in bed, where do you like to be kissed and what kind of verbal interaction you like to have. These are all details that create your sexuality. Just like everything else we have been 'talking' about, this is a subject that you have to understand and master.

You need to know your body, listen to it, see what makes you feel good, explore on your own and most important, let go of any blockages that limit your sexual pleasure.

Just pay attention to how this subject makes you feel by reading about it; is it uncomfortable reading about you discovering your body and what makes it tick? Do you believe it's a sin or that is not ladylike?

If anything that you are reading doesn't feel good and makes you shy regarding this subject, then you have to look deeper and see why is that. Finding out why certain areas of the sex talk and sexuality subject makes you uncomfortable is critical. You need to find out what are your beliefs about sex and intimacy and work on them. Why? You already know that why is the best way to figure yourself out and see the deeper meaning and the belief you have been enforcing around sexuality.

Just like everything else, this is a process for some of you that want to live life in tune with yourself and be authentic.

Sexuality goes on these steps: knowing, exploring, embracing and experiencing.

See it as a strategy or a step by step process to understand more about your sexual energy and discover the preferences you have.

There is nothing difficult about it if you want to discover yourself even more or you would like to actually find out what is it that turns you on mentally and physically.

You need to know what you are into and most of us believe we do, but you still have to go exploring even more. There are still certain things and areas that you most probably didn't have the courage to explore and there is where you find out what else it is possible for you to enjoy.

Keep challenging your own body and mind. See what areas of your body are the most sensitive and where a touch feels best. Listen to your mind and explore fantasies, scenarios and surroundings. Find out what triggers your sexual side and how would you make those fantasies happen.

The best way of discovering yourself is by letting go of any judgment or criticism you hold for yourself. When you release that, you are free to experience and enjoy.

The more you explore the more you embrace your physicality and that is what we are aiming for. A sexual life, a positive energy-releasing sexuality that is noticed everywhere you go by everyone. Shine in every room you are getting int. Let your glow be seen!

The only way is by accepting and embracing everything about you, body and mind. Don't be ashamed to feel good, accept this natural human need and believe in its power. It really is your hidden weapon.

Never let go or ignore your sexual energy because it makes you shine, create, live, love. I don't believe you ever heard of someone having a healthy sexual life and being depressed or having suicidal thoughts. And that is because such thing is not possible. You just had the best sex ever and you feel like the end of the world is here and you have no reason to live. That is BS in capitals and it doesn't happen.

When You engage in this fun activity, there are 2 main hormones being released: oxytocin and endorphins; the "love hormone" and the pain killer.

It is a scientifically proven fact that the more sex you have, the happier you will be which means a better life quality and a better relationship.

So keep exploring and keep entertaining yourself, for a better mental and physical health, a better life.

Sex is health!

Sex is something that happened for you and me to be here, on this planet. The act consummated. I want to believe that everyone celebrates the fact that your parents had sex and had you as their baby.

Sex is not just a procreation act; sex is the deepest form of intimacy between 2 people where you share more than just physical contact. Sex is something that needs to be enjoyed, respected and appreciated. This is what makes people connect, share, care for each other and burn some calories.

Sex is like food or sleep, it is a basic need that we have to meet for a better quality of life.

Mindset work: how do you feel about sex? Are you uncomfortable talking about it? Do you think sex it's dirty? Was it sex a taboo subject in your house or amongst friends? Did you have anyone to talk to about sex when you were younger?

I am no sex expert but the little I know is that if you consider sex only as a way of procreation, you will never experience the fun times and the enjoyment that comes with it.

Sex is beneficial for your mental health, boosts your immune system, creates stronger emotional bonds between partners, makes you shine, reduces the risk of heart problems and is proven to slow down the aging.

You have no reason not to want to have sex.

Think about your future, your life ahead; do you want to have an unfulfilled sexual life where things are just ok, routinely, just once in a while or do you want to enjoy every moment of it in this one life that we live on this planet? The answer is simple and the time for that decision is now. You don't want to waste any more of your time by having boring intercourse, that just a man it's supposed to need and don't fully enjoy it. Life is too short not to embrace your sexuality and not to have a happy sexual life. This is the only way we can differentiate friends from intimate partners, sex is what makes the difference. When you choose a life partner this is a very important subject you need to pay attention to because you are choosing someone that you are going to be intimate with, not just a help in the house, a financial source, a business partner, a friend or a 'good genes' subject. You are going to have sex with the person you chose to be with, so make sure you are connecting on this level and both of you have each other's interest in enjoying your intimate life.

This is one of the main reasons people are cheating, separating and divorcing. As much as it's a physical act, in fact, affects your emotional side most.

Never give up on this natural, normal pleasure, know yourself, explore, embrace your sexuality and keep experiencing. Have a happy sex life!

Keep glowing!

Chapter V

Relationships

Have you heard the affirmation *"the quality of your life is the quality of your relationships"*?

Take some time to think about it because it is 100% right. Our lives are being dictated by the type of relationships we have with the people around us. The relationships you have are deciding the success of a whole package woman. We have interactions and we bond with everyone around us; from the person at the grocery shop to the friend we have known for years.

Relationships are one of the most important areas of your life as it says the most about you, based on who you associate yourself with. It all starts with the relationship you have with your family, moving to your friendships, advancing into the work/study based network, to your private -intimate life.

The whole package woman engages in all of them and it's never part of conflicts, lost connections or gossips.

The whole package woman loves it's own parents no matter what and keeps in touch with the most important members of the family to her. She has friends she knows for years, that keeps in touch with and she is building new relationships in every environment she is in.

Work relationships are professional, caring and thoughtful and everyone is extremely happy to be working with such a high class and hard worker like you.

The whole package woman is living its own relationship on her own terms, by the couple's decisions and it's not being influenced by outside rules.

When it comes to intimate relationships, there is one scene in one movie that I believe it enhancing our own feminine nature and interest in this matter. That would be Julia Roberts in Eat

Pray Love where she goes to Bali at the beginning of the movie to meet this wise man and understand his wisdom deeper. She can talk to him about anything she wants and ask him any question about life. And the question she is asking is related to her own relationship (marriage). It is a funny scene because it portrays how much we are interested in this particular subject.

If you think about the conversations you have with your closest friends, they are predominantly about your love life. Of course, things change and priorities move in the hierarchy, but we still get really excited talking about relationships and love.

So, basically ladies this is a subject we absolutely love discussing because we like to analyze, we love to rethink everything and sharing private matters makes us bond.

There is nothing bad about it because most of the time sharing private subjects helps us to connect to each other, to receive advice, to help others by sharing our own experience and most importantly, to get someone to listen to what we have to say.

Let me ask you a question: do you believe in happily ever after? Do you believe that people can be loyal and happy together until death do them part?

This is the main thing! This is when you see your own fixed mindset and I cannot stress how important it is to know this about yourself.

We have all been raised with an example of a family type, we all experienced different relationships on our own or have seen friends going through stages in their relationships. That is what shaped our opinion about these kinds of connections. Is it what you witnessed and or experienced making you believe in life long relationships or is negatively impacted you?

Can you say that you had the best example of relationship and marriage in your family and everything has always been great? If yes, I am so happy for you because you can see that is possible to have a great connection with someone for a long time.

If not, and it's the most scenarios, then what is stopping you from learning more?

That was exactly what I asked myself when I started working with 2 relationship coaches at once. I knew that I didn't have the best marriage example of my life coming from my parents, as they divorced when I was really young and coming out of my 3rd serious, long term relationship with a broken heart, I needed to do some things differently; to save myself some time of learning on my own, I got the people that already studied all of that to help me out.

Said and done and it helped tremendously.

My new mindset became positive when it comes to a great relationship and I can see the possibility in that happening. There is work to be done prior to that, self-work, but the benefits and value that will add to both partners will be infinite.

When we start looking for a life partner or if there is already someone in our lives, we need to understand some basic facts about that.

We would never fall for someone that resembles bad on us, that is normal or basic, even cheap or below our own self-value because if that happens, it is exactly what it would say about us. We have a craving of idealizing and fantasizing about the other half.

I am not a relationship expert but as my top skill is learning, I can tell you that I had 2 relationship coaches and I have learned many things from them, as well as applied them.

I have failed relationships from friends to boyfriends, the plan is to learn how to manage them better, sustain the old friendships and succeed in the next relationships.

Just like everything else you have to choose in life, a friend and a partner is something we have to choose. We cannot just settle for what comes our way unless we know emotionally and rationally is the right fit for us.

Let me break a fixed mindset and affirmation I have been hearing all my life. That is opposites attract, which is absolute bullshit.

OPPOSITES DON'T ATTRACT!

Unless you are a magnet, you can't be attracted to the different pole.

People that share values in common, interests, passions, visions, moral standards and even physical traits are the ones that get together successfully.

These are character traits, personalities, which make us who we are and determine what we are attracted to.

If you know this about yourself, you will much easier find the people you want to be surrounded by and find yourself a life long partner.

That is if you want to share your life with someone, which most of the women out there want. Everything you desire from work to relationships starts by knowing yourself; so get yourself working and finding out all the above about you.

Just think about this for a second, if you are whole package woman, you need a whole package partner; but your whole package is different from the other person's whole package. You can do the same when it comes to the person you want to be with, think about the main areas of a package and define each chapter for the other person.

Why should you do this?

Primarily because when you are not happy with the other from the beginning and you compromise, those things will come back and haunt you. In the beginning, of course, life is great and roses are red, but those little things that you say that don't matter, they actually do. The way the other person dresses, or talks, or the friends they have, or the height, or their job, or their nose, or their views for the future; any kind of aspect in the package that is opposite than yours or not in accordance with what you want, will temporarily be ok, but long term destructive.

Do you really want to get into a relationship and have it destroyed, break hearts, waste time, just to find out it didn't work out because of character differences that you knew about, from the beginning?

We do make our own decisions based on emotions, but in all these cases we have to look rationally deeper to deal with them. If you know what you want and you have the portrait of the other one, but it doesn't quite fit, are you willing to put up with it and never mention it or complain about it?

It's not science when it comes to relationships, it's all about knowing yourself, knowing the other, active listening and a shared future vision.

What happens when we don't logically asses the other 'half'?

I have been guilty of one of the things I mentioned above, I have been in a couple of relationships since high school and I never truly thought about what I wanted and I can say that I failed those relationships because there were certain things that I wasn't fond of and closed my eyes, or simply thinking like a woman (I can change that about 'him').

Guess what, that never happened; so you can say I failed twice, the relationships and my commitment to myself that I will ignore that particular thing or change that person.

I was in a relationship for exactly 8 months with a great guy. He was 10 years older, very handsome, taller than me, fit, interested in creating a better future, good relationships with his family, but I couldn't stand his friends. Not that they were bad people, but the parties they were having, the music they were listening to, the subjects they were engaging in, the relationships values they were having; so, I decided he is great and his friends don't matter. Well, they did, since the time we were not spending together, he was spending it with them and in most of the social circumstances, they were present. I couldn't fit in because I didn't want to since I didn't agree with many of the things they were interested in.

So there it goes, 8 months of life with a great person that I couldn't be with in the long term. I didn't waste my time because I am here at this moment understanding my needs, wants, values and package. You truly fail the relationships when you keep doing the same things and going in consciously blind with a perception that you will get it all sorted along the way.

That can happen in business and at work, but the price you pay when it comes to relationships is much greater, as there are time and feelings spent on it.

What if you can see the other person as your perfect package, but proves to be the wrong fit for you? That can happen and the other person may conceive some traits they are aware are unattractive or even repulsive. Your job when you meet someone new is to leave that date with at least 3 new things you found out about them. Ask questions, especially about the things that you are interested in and see their opinion and mindset when it comes to that subject; observe them in the smallest of things and reflect afterward what that says about that person.

Let's take a recent example of my life; dinner with this great guy I am fond of: waiter comes with the menu and we start looking for what we prefer. A couple of minutes later I know my drink and my food preference; the waiter comes over and takes the drinks order, but gives us more time for the food as my date wasn't ready. Nearly 10 minutes passed after we received the drinks and he couldn't decide what he wants to eat. It's the seventh time or more when we are dinning in this particular restaurant and we still wait for him to decide the food he wants to eat.

I, obviously, helped with the food choices, but this particular scene which it's not a big deal or is ignored by others told me something important.

He is very indecisive as if he does that with food, he will do it in life matters as well. What should I do? The lesson is learned and the plan stands like this: when the moment comes and I would like this person to support me in a cause or to sell a vision for the future, I would have to give as little options as possible (to make it easier for him to decide) and to cover the 'what ifs' that will come from him and expose his personal gain.

Monogamy is a myth

The definition of monogamy is being married to one person at the time and zoology is exactly the same. So, the idea and the concept we have sold in our lives that monogamy is one person for life is completely wrong. It does exist in other countries with strict religions, but I am quite interested in finding out how many of those marriages everyone is really fulfilled and doesn't crave or fantasize about anyone else.

It might have been some successful ones and I would love to hear their story and that might help really and truly believe in destiny, as a hidden power that controls people's future.

Monogamy it really is one person at the time and staying faithful to the one you choose in your life, not the bs that we are supposed to be only one person for life.

So, I suggest everyone that is in min number 2 relationship to redefine their status of being monogamous.

All the relationship work will start with you, by knowing what you want and understand what you need in the other person.

Start working on your relationship needs, on your partner's traits in the package and don't settle for less.

Define each chapter with what you need the other person to be in order for you to love, cherish, stay faithful forever. In matters of looks: are you attracted to skinny, fit, tall, short, blue eyes, brunettes, etc? Know that about yourself, see how you feel when certain people are around you, look at your passed crushes and what you liked in matters of physical traits about them.

When it comes to interests and passions; what is it that you connect on with the other person on a deep level? What makes your conversations spark and how are you bringing ideas and intellectual challenges on those subjects?

Work-wise; are you both doing things for money that you absolutely love? What are your plans for the future and how is your life going to look like in 10-20 years from now?

Relationships: is the other person a loner or an extrovert? What about their circle of friends? Are they pushing him/her forward and helping out or are their morals questionable? What about the family ties, relatives and bonds created a long time ago? Is she/he maintaining those or he/she forgot about the first kind of love we have been thought since birth?

Mindset work: is the other a positive or a negative person? Is it someone that forgives others easily or tends to hold a grudge? Does she/ he likes change and progress or she/he prefers to settle in the current position? Does he/she have aspirations for the future or believes that just the fortunate ones make it in life?

There are many things to think about but you definitely have to consider these aspects otherwise you will find yourself going in one direction and the other one in a completely different one. And not just that; it will be time wasted, feelings hurt, frustration and resentment that will turn into despising the other one.

Another mindset and fixed belief I would like to disrupt is the one regarding children.

I cannot count how many times I have been hearing women saying "I am getting old, I should have kids", "I am turning 30 and no children yet", "I want kids before I am 35".

How comes in a modern era with so much technology around us, with so many individuals considering themselves open-minded, we are still operating on such a dated belief?

Stop being selfish when it comes to kids!

It's simple: a child is all about that child, it's not about you.

It's not about reaching a position in that firm, is not about feeling ready, is not about reaching six figures, is not about locking down a partner, it's not about starting a new hobby or even having someone that loves you unconditionally.

A child is all about that human being.

So, if you found yourself saying something similar to my statements above, or even think about that, start reassessing the reasons you are contemplating on that matter.

The main areas to think about when it comes to bringing a baby into your life are: your relationship status and the quality of it, your financial situation, your emotional 'fitness', the environment you are living in, the relationships you have with your family and the ones close to you, the quality of life, your time to dedicate to its bringing up and the main lessons you want it to learn about life.

Let's start with the relationship aspect; you are not in a happy and healthy relationship if you can't say without thinking that you want your partner to be the co-parent and you can't see a future with them; it means it's not the time to have a baby. The most important aspect of having a baby is who you are going to have that baby with. If there is no trust, support and responsibility, you will raise a child in a broken family, mostly being a single mum and a toxic environment that will damage the child's future, if the father is not around.

Financially, there are more costs involved in raising a child than you think about. The child itself doesn't need money, but everything from giving birth to raising it, it means extra expenses. Are you ready to cover everything that a child needs from a financial point of view?

Emotionally, how is it that you consider yourself? Do you have a quick temper? Are you anxious or depressed? Do you see the implications of you not being emotionally fit to have a baby at the right moment, if you are considering? A child will always do what you are doing and learn from you, not what you say but the example you are giving.

Will talk to itself the way you talk to yourself, will engage in the same activities as you do and will be prone to experience the same moods and reactions as you.

Will your home be your baby's home as well. How is it everything designed? Is it baby safe? Will it have its own space? Who else is living with you and how can they influence your child?

Your family becomes its family as well. Do you have a good relationship with your relatives? Will your child get to know its grandparents? What is the contribution that your family has on raising your baby?

One thing that kids need is time. That time that you spend with them will turn into memories. How much time do you have to raise your child? What about getting some help, like a nanny? How do you think a day in your baby's life would look like?

Last but not least, you must have an idea of how would you like that child to be like; if you considered having one. What are his main traits? What is it important to you that you are going to teach? What lessons about life will you transmit to the next generation?

This part has been structured on questions for a specific reason. I am not giving anyone lessons on how to raise a baby, but these questions will help you understand how ready you are to have one, raise it in a healthy environment and understand the responsibility you are about to take on.

For those who already have a child and things are not particularly ok and some of the points mentioned above have been disrupted in some way or another, you can make it work!

There are out there like-minded moms and women that go through similar challenges that you might encounter, make sure you help and support each other. In the end, this is what we have in life, we have each other, individuals that want the same thing, the best for its own child that will go great lengths for their wellbeing. Put aside jealousy, comparison and feelings that blind your decision making progress, take a step back and look at the bigger picture. I have seen many mums that get into an agreement with other mums because they cannot see beyond the perfection of their baby. Be rational and think things through, as whatever it is that you encourage will go down the line in the next generations.

This chapter was an intense one for me as I am determined to change something in women's mindset that says not to leave 'love' in the hands of fate. Reassessing your personal life will take some time; if you are not in a relationship I am convinced this will help you greatly; if you already are in one, start looking at the different aspects that compose that relationship and remember that you cannot change people but you can influence them, by being an example.

Chapter VI

Wealth

"Wealth is like a fruit tree"
Carlos slim Helu

I couldn't t describe wealth better than this. There are many definitions out there on what wealth is but nothing as explicit as this. Wealth is not just money, not just business, not just income, not just property. Wealth covers all of it and it is about building the life of your dreams by taking care of this main thing.

As we already covered the riches when it comes to health, relationships, spirituality, mindset, this chapter will focus on the creation of wealth and legacy.

I wouldn't say have your own definition about wealth as we might get it wrong; I suggest looking at wealth as the person I mentioned above sees it-like a fruit tree. Wealth is having that tree that constantly produces fruits and has no seasons for fruc-tification. Wealth would be the accumulation of assets. It would be a fruit or more from each asset class that doesn't ever stop growing.

Wealth is measured in fixed and liquid assets. (money, property, stocks, bonds, etc).

Now, that we talk about money I want you to think about what are your believes about money. Most of us have been brought up with the idea that money is the root of evil and money doesn't make you happy.

We have been told that since we were tiny creatures; but do we believe it? Look at your actions and see if you are behaving with your finances that way. Have a close look to see if you find yourself saying those things. We have discussed about mindset being the key in everything you desire in life, so what's your mindset on money?

Let me tell you what's my mindset: money is the tool that allows me to do the things I enjoy in life with the people I want. I love money and what it can do for me.

In the end, money is just plastic or paper and it has the value we give it. There is nothing good or bad about money, is just a number or a note. But in order for you to get more, you need to start liking it, enjoying it, valuing it; you can't expect thinking negatively about it and wanting it into your life at the same time. it's like saying "that person is so bad to me, but I want to spend more time with it"; If you think this way you will see how money disappear from your sight, not through magic, but you will find plenty of ways to dispose yourself from it; there will always be something to spend your last couple of hundred on and it's just because you can't keep money on you because you don't value it. Rethink the idea of money and challenge yourself to like it a little bit more than you did until now.

Money can actually make you a better person if you do the right things with it. You can free up your time by having more money, you can make better presents for the ones you love, it can help you travel and invest in your passions, you can even donate and help others in need. The more money you have, the more people you can help having a better life as well. People close to me know how important role adoption is in my future, that's why I know the more money I will be making-more lives I will change and richer my life will become from all the other aspects.

So, what are the main things you wish to accomplish by having more money? It's not about the note, it's about what you can do with that note. What is the value you attribute to that note?

What can you do with money to provide a better life for yourself and the ones close to you?

As soon as you figure out what you want to do with money and what money mindset you have to break, it's time to look at the ways you can produce more.

Nothing will ever be as valuable as you are, that's why I encourage everyone I meet and spend time with, to invest in themselves. Just like buying this book, it's an investment in yourself. There is no better way to spend money than spending it on your own growth and knowledge. By doing that you will add value to yourself, people around you will benefit from it and you will start earning more. You can choose courses, books, seminars, mentors, coaches.

Personally, I had all of them; I have done a number of courses, read a number of books (it never feels like too many), I attended seminars, I had life coaches and relationship coaches and I have business and property mentors.

Everything helped me in a way or another, starting off with mindset, working on personal stuff that was holding me back and starting a property business.

I struggled in the beginning with the idea of having mentors or paying people to guide me, as I am coming from a country that people want to get free information and do things on the cheap. I had to work on myself and look at those people's results to understand how much time they wasted, how much stress they had and how many mistakes they have done, just by not wanting to accept that they need coaching along the way. I am extremely happy to say that it didn't take me long to see all the benefits of having business mentors and as soon as I felt ready, I went for it.

If you can start doing something straight away is looking at what your blocks are, find someone that can help you get over that and take action to become financially free. Everything you want to do in life, there is someone else that has already done it. Save yourself years of learning, failing and losing money and pay someone to guide you step by step on how to achieve those things you desire. Nowadays, the university is something that gets you in debt and in a job. The idea is simple: are you going to study something that will take you minimum of 3 years or are you going to pay someone that is already where you want to be and spend less time getting there? You still cannot systemize medicine, law, science, but many of the other uni courses don't prepare you for what you have to face on a daily basis.

We need to have respect and appreciation for the people that have gone through all of those stages that we have been taught to follow, school, uni, job, marriage, etc; they are the people that spent time and money on learning something and getting into a job, that might or might have not been their passion or dream. That being said, if you are at a crossroads and you are planning to do something just for the sake of it (like going to study business), think twice as there won't be enough knowledge to get you ready for the real world and nothing that some manual says won't deal with the real issues you will be facing in that field.

Every business requires some simple things; it requires a number of people to serve, it needs to add value to its customers and it requires marketing.

I will give you a tip on the most important niches that will always make money if done it right.

1. Health
2. Wealth
3. Happiness

If you focus your business in any of these niches, the success rate will be extremely high. Find out what people want and give it to them. Provide that service that no one is providing or create a better one and market the hell out of it.

Take 'Beats' example; they are great headphones, but are they really the best? No matter what your answer is, everyone knows Beats as the top of headphones. There is market research done and Beats are not the top of the list; but, somehow the no.1 headphones, the best ones, are not something I heard of. People know Beats and that is because Jimmy Iovine has done a hell of a promotion when it came to their product. It doesn't matter which other headphones are better, what it matters is that when someone has got Beats, they make a statement, they support the company, they support the people that created them and also, they associate themselves with those people. This is one of the examples that proves a very important point: that marketing is key! There is nothing as important as that as soon as you have a product or a service. Social media made it really easy for us nowadays, anything we want to get out there, we can leverage all the platforms to get to the people that want what we have.

Your job won't make you rich!

I know you know that, but are you doing anything to change your status? Are you happy to retire at 50-60 or even 70? If the answer is no, and I really hope it is, what is it that you do to change that?

In my case I chose property, bricks and mortar, nothing sounds safer than that. Obviously, if you know what you are doing. I didn't know where to start, so I paid two experienced investors to teach me their strategies. Money well invested in myself and also in property by having the right education.

Statistics show that over 90% of the world's richest people have built their fortune through real estate. I will name you a few ways why that works so well.

Property will make you loads of money if done right.

One of the many ways it does that it's because of the appreciation. If you know your market and buy the right properties, in time their value will grow. Take UK's case for example: every 10 years the property value has been doubling. So, is it good to invest in property? Absolutely!

Cashflow-another way in which you create wealth through property. 'Cashflow is king' like papa GC would say. The main thing on creating cashflow is making sure the running costs are lower than the income each property is making, so every month you will have a source of cash that goes into your pocket after everything else is being paid. This is what an asset is-doing the job once and getting paid forever.

You can also do what is called "forced equity", which is the first thing I have done in property. By doing this you add value to the property, like adding a new bedroom, extra bathrooms, My first deal was converting a one-bedroom flat into a two-bedroom flat, with no experience, no building knowledge, but by having the right education and people around to guide me.

Think money-making property, not a perfect home, if you want to create wealth through property.

Property is a numbers game; if the numbers don't work, move to the next one; emotions have no place in this game.

One more reason property will make you rich is due to inflation. The value of money is decreasing, so money in your bank won't have the same value they have now, in one year's time. What it doesn't change and it actually increases is the goods that people pay for. So, when rents and property value it's increasing, you will be the one benefiting from it, if you do the right thing today.

These are the main reasons I choose property for myself as an investment and a wealth creation strategy. And also, because weirdly, I like to see floor plans and I really like to see the transformation that can happen to a property; but no more than that, I like to see money coming in without me doing any hard work, as it is so easy to leverage everything.

If I didn't get you convinced on why you should invest in property, come to an event with my two amazing mentors in London and you will see real people making money in the easiest ways.

s I have covered the whole package woman and we went through all the steps, now is time for you to get your mind and focus on the right things and start working on the things that you desire.

I want to make sure you get the main things out of this book and so, I wrote one chapter.

I came out with this last chapter quite late, but it's of great importance.

It will focus on the main mindset changes that I worked on throughout the book and it will help with your daily plan of action.

1. *You can be and have everything you desire*

You have all the tools within yourself to make any dream become a reality. You are structured in the same way as any other person that 'made' it. You are enough! You have it all! Remember that quitting on your dreams won't actually bring you the life you envisioned. Stop finding excuses for yourself and don't justify your lack of confidence or low self-worth. You can be anything you would like to! And you can have absolutely anything in life! Believe in yourself!

2. *Self-love and self-care is not selfish*

Learn that your own happiness and health come first. If

you are at your best, everyone around has a lot to benefit from. If you constantly compromise and prioritize everyone else around you, but yourself, you will never achieve your dreams and even more important, you will never be someone that others want to follow.

Take care of yourself so you can take care of others. You would want the ones close to you to look after themselves and have a better life and health, so don't forget that you show them an example; make sure they see in you the way to treat themselves.

3. *Knowing yourself is the root of wisdom*

This is actually a quote that I really love, that comes from Aristotel "knowing thyself is the beginning of all wisdom"

It speaks the truth; the more you learn about yourself, evolve your mind, learn about your mindset, analyze your behavior patterns, keep close attention to your emotions and reactions- the more you can identify these in people and know how to interact with them.

There is no greater achievement than understanding yourself, knowing yourself on a deeper level and not judging what you find out. It requires power and courage to look at yourself and accept everything you are, with 'good and bad'

4. *Set goals so high that make you uncomfortable*

Remember that any goal that you would consider 'quite easy' to get won't make you take action. We are mostly taking decisions and acting based on feelings, we are emotional creatures; your dreams have to give you shivers and make you so excited that you can't wait to live another day to get a chance to get closer to them.

5. *Start with the end in mind*

The end is your vision, your destination, your biggest goal. It represents the ultimate thing you want to achieve in life. When you wake up in the morning and you see yourself where you are heading in a few year's time, nothing will feel hard. Always keep the bigger picture with you as it helps to keep you on the right track and follow through with your purpose.

6. *A pat on the shoulder is a kick forward*

After every achievement make sure you stop for a second and interiorize what just happened. Life is not a race for the next best thing and you will never be pleased with anything unless you appreciate where you got so far. Understanding that will get you to the next level sooner than you think and you will be more fulfilled.

7. *What else can I do?*

Keep this question in mind. It has helped me throughout my life with everything I have done so far. Every fear I overcame, every deal I closed, every physical challenge I accomplished as it won't let me settle for just that. In the end, it is connected to our potential, not knowing what we are capable of and always striving to be and do better.

8. *Destiny is when your eyes are open to opportunities*

This is my own definition of destiny. I believe in things happening for us and having your eyes open. If you are closed and half awake, nothing will benefit you and all the opportunities will fade away as you won't see them. Keep your eyes open and see the benefits in each situation you are presented and take action; a well-lived life might be around the corner.

9. *Failure is just a matter of perception*

I have already spoken about failure a lot and the idea should be implemented within ourselves. Failure does happen to the ones that see it that way. If your own standard of failure it's represented by what others think about it, you will fail; if you change that and make it beneficial to you, see all the positives and learning lessons-you will not fail.
If you manage to that, and you will-the word failure will no longer be in your vocabulary.

10. *You have the power to transform your weaknesses into strengths*

This refers to all weaknesses non-related to skills. Emotional and intellectual weaknesses; the sooner you know and understand them, the earlier you will be able to change them into positives. Fear, self-doubt, lack of patience, lack of confidence, inadaptability; all of these can be changed or even better make them work for you. See the good it can actually bring you and change it in the way that it benefits you, not vice versa. It is possible.

11. Self-image sets the boundaries of performance in your life

Something that the greatest Maxwell Maltz said years ago. We need to pay so much attention to the way we see ourselves because that is the way we are going to be and act throughout our lives. If we believe about ourselves that we are positive, negative, impatient, confident, strong, silly, etc. that is the way we are going to take life on board. Be careful with the way you perceive yourself as it can make you or break you.

12. We are meant to be abundant in all areas

This is the main thing I want to spread across. We are not meant to have one or the other. Just being fit and in a great relationship, but with no money. Or a thriving business and great marriage, but no fullfilment and sickness in our body.

Life has given us all the tools to achieve everything we desire. You know how to get into great health, you have the resources on how to make more money and be finanacially free, you know if you want to get into a happy, healthy committed relationship; and you know if all these will make you fullfilled or not.

Don't settle for less than you can have, just because other people believe that.

Life is meant to be abundant in all areas.

I hope you enjoyed what I shared with you!

I can only hope you got inspired and influenced on making your life better and finding your purpose.

On the back of the book, there are 2 ways on how to get in touch with me. Also, I have started a FB Community designed only for women, to support and encourage each other.

FB group- The Whole Package Woman Community

I have also started using the following hashtags:

#thewholepackagewoman

#toobusylovinglife

#writingismarketing

Let's create a community of supporting women.

Let's create more whole package women!

Thank you!

Xoxo,

TWPW Rebeca

www.thewholepackagewoman.com

Lightning Source UK Ltd.
Milton Keynes UK
UKHW010726130421
381918UK00003B/493